Endorsements

Joyce and Cliff Penner have done it again! After decades of pioneering work in sexuality and after counseling thousands of couples, they get to the naked truth about sex like nobody else. Every woman—along with her husband—should read this insightful book. It will positively transform your love life.

DRS. LES AND LESLIE PARROTT
#1 *New York Times* best-selling authors of *Saving Your Marriage Before It Starts*

Joyce and Cliff Penner are two of the best thinkers and clinicians we know when it comes to the wonders of sexuality and intimacy. They are thoughtful, informed, biblical, straightforward, and compassionate. And the topic is inspired and much-needed. This book will bring joy, delight, help, and wisdom to everybody who reads it.

JOHN ORTBERG
Senior pastor, Menlo Park Presbyterian Church; author of *All The Places to Go*
NANCY ORTBERG
Author of *Seeing in the Dark: Finding God's Light in the Most Unexpected Places*

When I needed practical assistance to overcome the damage of childhood sexual molestation, Joyce and Cliff Penner were a godsend, and for more than twenty years, they have been mentors, models, and friends. *Enjoy!: The Gift of Sexual Pleasure for Women* elevates the needs, desires, and experiences of women as they embrace their sexuality in marriage. No one writes about sex with more passion, expertise, and wisdom than they do!

KAY WARREN
Cofounder of Saddleback Church, Lake Forest, CA

For any woman who is dissatisfied and discouraged with the physical intimacy in her marriage, *Enjoy!* contains a wealth of wisdom and practical advice that is sure to be helpful. The Penners understand the challenges common to wives, and I'm confident their latest book will help many couples experience a newfound joy and closeness as they follow this roadmap for mutual sexual fulfillment.

JIM DALY
President of Focus on the Family

JOYCE J. PENNER, M.N., R.N. & CLIFFORD L. PENNER, Ph.D.

ENJOY!
THE GIFT OF
SEXUAL PLEASURE
FOR WOMEN

TYNDALE HOUSE PUBLISHERS, INC.
CAROL STREAM, ILLINOIS

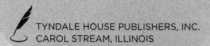

FOCUS ON THE FAMILY® | FOCUS ON MARRIAGE™

A Focus on the Family book published by Tyndale House Publishers, Inc., Carol Stream, Illinois 60188

To our three daughters:
Julene Stellato, child and adolescent psychologist; Carrie Walton
Penner, K–12 educational advocate; and Kristine Penner Klein,
gynecologic oncologist; who are at the juggling stage of life—
nurturing their children, living out their professions, giving to
and caring for others, while facing the challenge of finding special
moments to enjoy their husbands and take time for self-care.

Contents

Introduction *ix*

1. Enjoy *1*
2. Listen *17*
3. Lead *27*
4. Plan and Prepare *37*
5. Pleasure *47*
6. Talk *55*
7. Practice Intimacy *67*
8. Pursue Healing *77*
9. Embrace Differences *97*
10. Protect *115*
11. Accept Reality *123*
12. Keep Learning *131*

Appendixes *137*
Notes *155*
Additional Resources *159*
About the Authors *161*

Introduction

OVER OUR MORE THAN forty years as sex therapists and educators, we've come to realize that many assumptions about women and sex simply are not spot-on. And what's worse, they do not work well for a lasting, mutually enjoyable sex life in marriage.

There are plenty of ways to end up with these beliefs and practices, which do more harm than good. Personal history, culture, experience, and confusion regarding Scripture—all of these influences can lead to false assumptions about women and sex. While many of these ideas do contain a germ of truth, we've learned that often they are applied incorrectly.

Throughout this book, we'll share our observations and findings about women and sex. What we've learned and taught has made a positive difference in the sexual relationships between many husbands and wives. These findings have evolved over the years from the stories of thousands of individuals and couples who have come to us with disappointments or frustrations and have found relief and mutual fulfillment. It's our hope that you, too, can find that fulfillment.

Just as our goal in writing *The Married Guy's Guide to Great Sex* was to help men understand, accept, and fulfill their roles for sex in marriage, *Enjoy!* is meant to help women discover total acceptance and expression of their God-given sexuality as wives. We'll share how you, as a woman, can learn to embrace your sexual role in marriage and find more enjoyment with your husband.

In *The Married Guy's Guide to Great Sex*, we dispelled myths about men and sex, and shared how the husband is to love his wife as Christ loves us—unconditionally.

In *Enjoy!*, we'll clear up false assumptions about women and sex and empower you to embrace your unique sexuality and share all of who you are with your husband.

After you read this book, we encourage you and your husband to read it out loud together. As you read, stop to explain what describes you and what does not fit for you.

We trust there will be many deeply rewarding moments as you discover who you are as a sexual person and as you pursue full acceptance and expression of your God-given sexuality in your marriage.

CHAPTER I

ENJOY

MAGGIE MADE CLEAR during her first session with us that she was willing to engage in sexual therapy only to save her marriage. She adamantly declared, "I have zero interest and don't care if we ever have sex again!"

Six months later, she couldn't imagine life without sex.

What brought on this dramatic change? Through the sexual therapy process, Maggie learned to take in pleasure for herself, allow arousal, and have regular orgasmic release. She was now communicating with her husband about her sexual likes and dislikes.

Not only had their sex life become positive for both of them, but all aspects of their relationship had improved. And much to Maggie's surprise, the anxiety that had often zapped her energy for life had disappeared.

Whether you have zero interest in sex as Maggie did, or you simply want to improve this aspect of your relationship with your husband, realizing the wide-ranging benefits of sex is a good place to start. Envisioning these benefits can heighten your anticipation and enjoyment of sex.

Realize the Benefits

Just as Maggie did, when women discover who they are as sexual persons, pursue their sexuality with their husbands, and experience sexual fulfillment, they find new and increased vitality in *all* aspects of life, not just in bed.

Sex does more than make you feel good. It improves your health, helps you communicate more effectively, and raises your self-esteem. Sex enhances your immune system and cardiac functioning, reduces stress and pain, and keeps you connected, and emotionally balanced.

There is growing evidence that good sex, particularly sex in a loving, committed marriage, has the power to promote both physical and emotional health.[1]

Sex can relieve symptoms of arthritis, insomnia, chronic pain, muscular tension, and mood swings, according to Judith Sachs's study of the research on the benefits of sex. Keeping active in a healthy sexual relationship can help you communicate your desires. Healthy sexual behavior and intimacy is a way to experience a greater sense of wholeness and well-being.[2]

When women experience the benefits of sex for themselves, their expectations shift from sex as a duty that benefits the man to mutual pleasure. That shift is vital to women's *and* men's sexual enjoyment.

Seek Enjoyment

Sex is not a gift women give to their husbands, but rather one they enjoy for themselves and share freely with their husbands. When the woman pursues and learns to enjoy sex, both spouses will be pleased with their sex life. We encourage you to pursue enjoyment rather than "do your duty."

When Joyce speaks to Mothers of Preschoolers (MOPS) groups, she finds that so many of the women have lost the enjoyment of sex and have fallen into a routine of "doing their duty." It takes sex to make children, yet children sap our energy for sex.

Here's the question she often hears: "How do you get in the mood when you're not in the mood, and don't even want to be in the mood?"

Her answer? "You don't have to be in the mood or even want to be in the mood; you can decide to have sex because you know it is good for you, not because it is your duty to do it for him."

Duty sex *won't* work for either of you for long; pursuing sex for you whether or not you are in the mood *will* work.

One mom expressed it so clearly: "Last time you were here, you talked about making time for sex even if I didn't feel like it. Since then, we have had 'regular' times and it has *completely* changed my heart and feelings and drawn us closer together as a couple. Thank you!"

Pursue enjoyment rather than "do your duty."

Instead of "doing her duty," the woman's role for sex in marriage is to pursue all of who she is sexually and share her sexuality with her husband. The prerequisite to fulfilling her role is for her to enjoy sex.

As Kathy so aptly expressed when we interviewed her and Pastor Joey for our *Magic and Mystery of Sex* videos: "I love it! What can I say?"

Do you love it? You may not love it, but is sex enjoyable for you? Is it good for you? If you are enjoying sex, we encourage you to continue fully embracing your sexuality with gusto. If you are not enjoying sex with your husband, it's important to understand why that might be true and how to find enjoyment.

Sex doesn't have to be ecstatic to be enjoyed. Many times women will think it should feel like it did when it was new and so exciting. As one woman asked in an e-mail to us: "I don't enjoy sex as much as I used to. How can I start feeling the 'spark' again?"

We encourage you to think about enjoyment this way: Consider "0" as neutral, "+10" as ecstasy (you can't imagine more enjoyable sex), and "-10" as misery (you'd like to run out of the room screaming). It's okay to engage in sex with your husband as long as it is neutral or above, but never let a sexual experience go below "0."

If you start having negative feelings, stop and invite any touch or activity that you have enjoyed or think you might enjoy—anything that replaces the negative sensations. As you learn to take responsibility to avoid negative feelings and increase positive sensations, you will experience greater enjoyment and even add a little spark now and then!

Look Back to Move Ahead

To begin your journey to find or increase your enjoyment of sex with your husband, it's helpful to explore your perceptions of sex and what contributed to them. Your answers to the following questions can help you pinpoint any obstacles in your path to enjoyment.

WHAT DO YOU THINK OF WHEN YOU THINK OF SEX?

Women come to marriage with a mind-set toward sex based on the family and culture they grew up in—the "messages" they received from their mother, siblings, friends, community, church, the media—as well as their unique set of exposures and experiences.

Whatever view of sex you brought to marriage, it's important to counteract any negative perspective with the positive anticipation of sex and its benefits, which were mentioned earlier. As you intentionally replace negative views with positive attitudes, you will increase your enjoyment of sex.

WHAT DID YOU LEARN ABOUT SEX GROWING UP?

Pause just a moment and think. Pay close attention to both the verbal and nonverbal messages you received.

Pay attention to the messages you received.

If there was no discussion or exposure to sexual viewpoints, you may have come to marriage with a fairly neutral perspective. If you heard healthy messages about God's wonderful design of sex and the joy it brings to marriage, you received a wonderful blessing. If the messages were negative, hopefully you were able to counter them before you were married. If not, you may have to undo and reprogram your mind-set.

Women who come to us for sexual therapy report having heard

messages such as: "It's your job to keep your knees together," "Never let anything in there," or "Never touch down there except to wash with a cloth." These messages were likely crafted to keep you from self-stimulation or from having sex before marriage.

If the warnings were not accompanied by teaching about the joy of sex in marriage, a woman isn't likely to differentiate between sex outside of marriage and sex within marriage. Sometimes these women come to us with unconsummated marriages. They still "haven't let anything in there."

Another teaching that negatively affects sex in marriage is that it is the woman's responsibility to set sexual limits before marriage, rather than the mutual responsibility of both partners. You may have felt responsible for getting the guy aroused by what you did or what you wore, so you never could enjoy your body and how it looked or felt. Women who took on the gatekeeper role in dating often continue to be the gatekeepers in marriage.

Subtle messages will also have influenced you. If there was a passionate kiss in a television show you were watching, how was that handled in your home? If your mother and father mutually enjoyed affection with each other, you likely will also. However, if your father was cold and distant or your mother pulled away if he was affectionate, you will have to be intentional in giving and receiving affection freely.

We hope you were raised with the teaching that sex is a good and wonderful gift to be enjoyed. If so, by the time you were a young adolescent you may have learned these five healthy attitudes:

- Sex is good and of God.
- Sexual curiosity is natural.
- Sexual responses are automatic.
- Responsibility for decisions about sexual actions belongs to both people in the relationship.
- Biblical standards and mutual respect are the guiding principles for all sexual choices.

WHAT WAS YOUR MOTHER'S VIEW OF SEX? WAS YOUR MOTHER A SEXUAL PERSON?

How you perceived your mother sexually will affect how you view yourself sexually. How your mother felt about herself as a woman and as a sexual person will have been communicated to you directly by what she taught you and indirectly as you observed the interaction between her and your father. As one woman expressed it: "After having kids I feel more like a mother than a wife. I struggle with switching from mother to lover." For her, motherhood was disconnected from being a wife and lover, which is likely what she sensed from her mother.

A woman will both actively reject what she heard from her mother and practice a different approach, or she will unconsciously accept what she heard and incorporate her mother's perspective as her own. What is true for you?

WHAT WAS YOUR FIRST MEMORY OF SEXUAL AWARENESS? SELF-DISCOVERY? EXPLORATORY PLAY? QUESTION ASKING?

You may have engaged in some exploratory play. You may have a memory of walking in on your parents making love, hearing something from a friend, or coming across some sexually explicit material even if it wasn't pornographic. Do you recall asking questions about sex, babies, or body parts? Do you remember any self-exploration when you tried to figure out your genitals?

HOW WAS YOUR PHYSICAL DEVELOPMENT HANDLED?

Every girl experiences the shift from having a girl's body to a developed body. For some the changes happen gradually, while others change quickly. How was that for you? Were you adequately prepared for your body shape changing, your feelings changing, your breasts developing, and obviously your first menstrual period? Or were you left on your own with those experiences? Maybe information about these changes came from your friends.

Were you one of the early ones in your group to develop, or were you behind your peers? Did you feel self-conscious, comfortable, inadequate, or different? If you developed early, before all the rest of your peers, you may have tried to hide your developing breasts by wearing baggy sweatshirts or slouching your shoulders. You may have been teased, made fun of, or been embarrassed.

Starting menstruation may also have been a positive or negative experience. If you were early or late to get your period, you may have felt different from your peers. If you had severe abdominal pain, headaches, or irritability, you may still have negativity and dread associated with your period. If you were well prepared and menstruation was expected as a positive sign of your maturation, you will likely have a better appreciation for being a woman.

Can you be proud that you are a sexual person?

What you experienced in the process of your physical development will have clearly affected your comfort with your body, as well as your view of sex. If you felt good about your sexual development, you are more likely to feel good about yourself as a sexual person.

Can you be proud that you are a sexual person? Is sex for you? If you believe being a sexual person is good and sex is for you, sex will be better for you and your husband.

DO YOU THINK WOMEN ENJOY SEX AS MUCH AS, MORE THAN, OR LESS THAN MEN? DO YOU ENJOY SEX AS MUCH AS, MORE THAN, OR LESS THAN YOUR HUSBAND?

IF YOU COULD REDO YOUR SEXUAL HISTORY, HOW WOULD IT BE DIFFERENT?

Would you ask more questions? Would you share more with your mother? Would you avoid engaging in certain activities? Would you talk more with your peers? Would you be more flirty and flamboyant, or less flirtatious? How would you like to have changed your life up to this point? If something had been different, would you feel better about yourself as a woman? What would that difference be?

Even though your history is what it is and is not in your control, you *can* take control of your adult sex life now by recognizing the positive and the negative impact of your history. You can maximize the positives and reframe the negatives, accepting that as an adult you are no longer a victim of your past.

Given the insights you have gained through this reflection, what are you hoping to find in this book? How do you hope the information will make a difference for you?

Characteristics That Increase Enjoyment of Sex

Now that you've taken time to reflect on your ideas about sex and what may have contributed to those ideas, you can take steps to find more pleasure.

Let's start by looking at the characteristics that we've found increase women's enjoyment of sex. Do you have realistic expectations? How connected are your sexuality and spirituality? Are you able to receive pleasure? Are you content with your body? Are you able to experiment with new ideas and allow flexibility? Are you free to say no to sex so that you can freely say yes to sex? Can you let go sexually?

Realistic Expectations

Couples preparing for marriage will make a much smoother transition to married life if they have clarified their expectations for sex with each other. Our book *Getting Your Sex Life Off to a Great Start*[3] is a great resource for helping premarital and newly married couples with that process.

Early in marriage, couples typically enjoy the excitement of a new relationship; the desire to be together sexually is spontaneous and frequent. As marriages age, children come along and other responsibilities tend to dominate. That's when expectations must change. It is essential that both spouses accept the need to make—and actually do make—the transition from newness, excitement, and infatuation to committed, lifelong intimacy.

Married love is a deeper, connected love. A 1987 study compared married love to the attachment process that happens in childhood. This study explored "the possibility that romantic love is an attachment process—a biosocial process by which affectional bonds are formed between adult lovers, just as affectional bonds are formed earlier in life between human infants and their parents."[4]

Married sex is not what we call "zap" sex, the kind you find in romance novels, movie sex scenes, or pornography. After being married for a while, you are not likely to feel like tearing his clothes off and making mad, passionate love when you meet at the end of the day.

A Yale study on love found that intense, initial passion dissipates six to thirty months after a new romantic relationship begins.[5] Those initial high-drive desires are fueled by the brain chemical dopamine, which is a powerful motivator or driving energy. As the brain production of dopamine decreases, the couple needs to shift to an attachment fueled more by the brain chemical oxytocin.

> Make the transition from infatuation to lifelong intimacy.

Oxytocin, which is associated with bonding, is released during hugging and pleasant physical touch, and plays a part in the human sexual response cycle. This oxytocin-fueled attachment is a deeper, binding love that lasts a lifetime. Yet the shift from large doses of dopamine to this oxytocin-fueled connection can feel like a loss.

Be assured: Desire isn't gone, it is just different. Nor have you lost your attraction to or love for each other. That also is just different! Embrace and enjoy the shift to a softer, more subtle urge for closeness and touch. After fifty-three years of marriage, we can promise you it is wonderful!

Spiritual Affirmation

When sexuality and spirituality affirm each other in your marriage, your enjoyment of sex will increase. But you may have difficulty enjoying sex in marriage if you learned to split your belief system from your sexual actions while you dated. Couples who allow this split find it's not as easy later on to integrate their sexuality with their spirituality.

We've seen many couples whose sexuality and spiritually were not aligned. They've come to us in preparation for marriage, saying they believe in waiting until marriage to consummate their sexual relationship. In fact, they will tell us they are saving sexual intercourse for marriage.

Yet when we ask more specifically if they have ever had intercourse, they will say, "Well, not really." As we ask more questions, we discover that this might mean that they aren't *intending* to have sex. Even so, it's happening "by accident" and regularly. Or they may be withdrawing before he ejaculates. Or they may have promised not to kiss before marriage, so they have never kissed but are having intercourse.

Pray with your husband about your sex life.

There are many versions of the way the split between beliefs and actions can happen and disrupt the integrated growth of sexuality and spirituality.

Whatever your situation, we encourage you to actively integrate your sexuality with your spirituality. Thank God for creating you as a sexual person; thank Him for sexual feelings and responses; pray with your husband about your sex life. Invite God into your sexual experiences with your husband. Read the Song of Solomon in the Bible and read a book, such as our *Gift of Sex*, out loud together to connect Scripture's affirmation of sexual enjoyment in marriage with your sexual experiences.

Ability to Receive Pleasure

Many times women are givers and haven't learned or allowed themselves to accept compliments, to soak in touch, or to receive sexual stimulation. A woman's ability to receive pleasure depends on how she feels about herself. Good self-esteem helps women feel worthy of receiving good things. How do you feel about yourself? Are you able to receive? What would help you to receive sexually?

Use our "Inhibition to Freedom" chart to help you grow in this area. On the left side of the diagram, write your difficulty with receiving pleasure; on the right side of the diagram, describe true freedom to receive pleasure as you would like to experience it.

Next, fill in the steps, breaking down your desired actions and necessary changes into "just noticeable differences." Practice the first step until you feel totally free receiving at that level. Then move to the next step. It's like pouring concrete steps; it's necessary to let the concrete cure before pouring the next one. If you can't take a step as you defined it—if it is too big—break it down until it's manageable for you.

Inhibition to Freedom

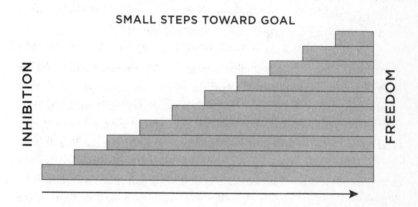

Here's how one woman in counseling used this system to gain freedom. Because she was not receiving pleasure, her husband felt more pressure to please her sexually. The pressure was making it difficult for him to respond sexually. She was focused on how he was doing, rather than on her own enjoyment. This was a lose-lose situation.

Her "inhibition" on the left of the chart was her discomfort or inexperience with accepting pleasure. To reach "freedom," she would take the first step on the chart—allowing her husband to caress her foot. Her task was to focus only on what felt good to her. She found that difficult at first; she kept wondering if he was enjoying it. So they were assigned that first step a number of times until she was able to trust him to take responsibility for himself and allow her to receive his caressing of her feet for her pleasure only.

Once she mastered the foot caress, other body touching was added. Her ability to relax and soak up the good feelings of being touched freed him to enjoy her body for his pleasure and lowered his performance pressure. It was a win-win!

Body Acceptance

Women are more likely to feel good about themselves when they like their bodies. And they are more likely to enjoy sex when they feel good about themselves. It is also important that how we look is in sync with who we are—our outside is representative of our inside.

Genesis 2:25 says, "And the man and his wife were both naked and were not ashamed" (NASB). Before sin, man and woman were totally open with God and with each other's bodies. When they disobeyed God, they were estranged from Him and covered their genitals. For the first time they felt shame. Now through Christ's redemption, we can connect with God and freely give our bodies to each other in marriage *without* shame.

Yet in our society, so much value is placed on women to have a culturally ideal body. The message is that a woman needs a certain type of body to be sexy. When there is a gap between how a woman views herself and the "ideal" body, it's difficult for her to enjoy sex. To accept her body and freely enjoy sex, it is essential that she close this gap. She can do this by adjusting her ideal. She can also take steps to modify her body through exercise, changes in eating patterns, and grooming.

When you think about your body or look in the mirror, with or without clothes, how do you feel about yourself? Does your view of your body fit with that of your ideal? The greater the gap between how you see yourself and how you would like to look, the greater your body image dilemma.

How might you close the gap between your view of yourself and your ideal? A great resource is *The Body God Designed: How to Love the Body You've Got While You Get the Body You Want* by Gregory L. Jantz.[6]

You might also use the steps diagram on the previous page to define on the left how you view yourself and on the right your ideal. Then you can fill in the steps from left to right. But first, you may need to change your ideal. So you might redefine your ideal on right side and not have so many steps to achieve to reach your goal.

The most common body image issue women in our culture fight is weight. A woman's ideal weight may not be realistic for her body structure, so we first help her define an achievable goal on the right side of the steps. She may need the help of a nutritionist or physician to determine what is realistic for her.

Once a reasonable goal is defined, we help her look at her lifestyle, habits, psychological issues, and other factors that might be preventing her from reaching her goal. We've discovered that women in this situation frequently get stuck because they hope to jump from where they are to their ultimate goal. We help them define small steps and find success at the first step before tackling the next.

Praying this prayer can also help you accept your body:

God, grant me
the serenity to accept the things about my body I cannot change,
the courage to change the things I can for the better, and
the wisdom to know the difference and get on with my life.[7]

Embracing New Experiences and Allowing Flexibility

Newness excites; flexibility brings freedom. Can you give yourself permission to experiment? You may need to solidify your ability to receive pleasure and the other previous characteristics before you attempt new experiences and push yourself to be flexible. Enjoy what is good for you right now. Many women want the comfort of their love play to include the expected activities they know they enjoy. When you can count on that solid base, you can nudge yourself to positively anticipate something new and creative if the steps to the newness are gradual. Keep your husband in the loop.

Ability to Say No

Women who can energetically say yes to sex are those who are free to say no. To be free to give yourself sexually, you must be free to make that choice. God offers us a relationship with Him through Christ's death and resurrection. He gives Himself to us with open arms, but He never *demands* that we accept His gift of love. It is freely our choice. It's a gift of ourselves to Him when we accept His gift to us. Likewise, when husbands love their wives as Christ loves us, they give themselves with open arms, but never demand a yes.

How a woman says no to sex with her husband is equally important. Men are human and can feel rejected. Be sure to be gracious in your response: Let your husband know that you recognize and understand his need. It is most helpful if both spouses are free to express their desire without demand that the other have the same level of interest. If you aren't interested, offer an alternative:

- "What if we get more rest tonight and plan a time for tomorrow?"
- "What if you get home a little earlier tomorrow and help with the kids (or dinner or something else)?"
- "I could enjoy some snuggle time and see where that leads, as long as there isn't pressure that it has to go all the way."
- "I would love to pleasure you as long as I don't have to get into it for myself."
- "I would love being pleasured but don't have the energy to pleasure you. What if we plan for your turn next time?"

The Power of a Positive No by William Ury is a great resource that teaches how to extend respect to each other while standing up for your self-interest and building a mutual relationship. Ury's writing is engaging, his examples blend a wonderful variety of experiences, and he extends great warmth in his teaching about how to handle differences. He shares practical reminders of how to consider the other person's perspective while gracefully asserting your own position to create a clear path to a win-win situation.

Ability to Let Go

Can you get into the moment—lose control and allow arousal, ecstasy, and orgasm? Can you let go of the minutiae of life, the tensions of the day, the pressures of the next day, the things you can't control? Can you savor the moment?

> For passion in marriage,
> a woman needs to be able to take;
> she needs to believe she is worthy of his affirmation
> and
> has the right to be intensely sexual.[8]

> She has to be able to enjoy her sexuality,
> her husband's sexuality, and
> her husband's enjoyment of her sexuality.
> Sex has to be as good for her as it is for him
> if it is going to be good for both for their lifetime.[9]

The best gift a woman can give herself, her marriage, her children, and her husband is her deep and real enjoyment of sexual times with him.

CHAPTER 2

LISTEN

To PURSUE ALL of who you are sexually and share your sexuality freely with your husband, you'll need to listen to your body. Your body will guide you if you learn to listen to it.

You might be wondering what we mean by "listening to your body." When I (Joyce) was in first grade, the teacher asked us to put our heads on our desks, close our eyes, and tell the class what we saw. The tighter I closed my eyes, the blacker it became; I saw nothing but darkness! You might be turning up your hearing aid but still aren't "hearing" anything. Don't be discouraged—you *can* learn to hear what your body is telling you.

To help you understand this concept, let's use an analogy. What happens when you are hungry? Do you notice little twinges of hunger before you really need to eat? Or do you just suddenly notice that you are ravenous for food? If you are around children, you will find that some are too interested in life to notice their hunger for food, while others seem to always be eager to eat.

Likewise, men and women are all wired with varying sensitivity to their bodies' sexual hungers. It's also possible that a person's innate sexual signals may be blocked by life events.

If you've accepted and affirmed God's design of you as a sexual person with all of the intensity He intended for you, you may already be in tune with your body's sexual messages. If you do not know how to listen, here are some suggestions that have helped other women. These tools may help you to increase your body-listening skills too.

> Good sex doesn't just happen, but you can make it happen by listening to your body.

- *Listen all day long.* Listen when you are falling asleep, waking up in the morning, in the shower, exercising, driving in the car, riding a bus, on an airplane, working on your computer, or shopping for groceries.

- *Listen to the little flickers.* These may be flickers of sexual sensations, genital tingles, need for touch, urge to be close, or desires for connection.

- *Listen while kissing.* Listen to how you like to kiss, and lead with your level of enjoyment while your husband follows your lead. Kiss lightly; kiss sweetly; kiss tenderly; kiss passionately.

- *Listen during sex.* During cuddling or touching times with your husband, practice going inside yourself and concentrate on listening to your body.

To increase your body-listening skills, it's important to have knowledge of five essential areas: your body, your sexual triggers, your brain, your hormones, and your potential. Let's start with the body.

Listen to Your Body by Knowing Your Body

Women are created to be sexually responsive. Our understanding of anatomy, physiology, our brains, and Scripture all affirm women's design for sexual responsiveness. You may be a woman who knows this as a reality for yourself, you may be one who experienced this at some point in your life but now don't, or you may be a woman who is upset with us for this teaching because you have never enjoyed sex. You may be angry with God and with us. We encourage you to read this section, whatever your situation.

To pursue sexual enjoyment for yourself and share your sexuality with your husband, it's important that you know the physical facts, as well as your unique body. Even as physical bodies are designed to work in all ways, not just sexually, some enter the world with sensory or other functions impaired or lose function because of some event in their lives. This can be true sexually as well. People with limitations or physical difficulties will likely require adaptations to experience life as fully as possible.

> Both win when the woman learns to listen to her body and goes after what she needs while the man listens to her and responds to her desires.

So let's first address how women's bodies are designed. A newborn girl lubricates vaginally within the first twenty-four hours after birth, even as a newborn boy has an erection within the first five to ten minutes of birth (as measured by Masters and Johnson researchers[1]). We as women typically are a little slower in our responses than men. Some say women are like a slow cooker; men are like a microwave. But you and your husband may be the opposite—there are always exceptions to the generalizations about male-female differences.

Adult healthy women also lubricate vaginally every eighty to ninety minutes while they sleep.[2] This is true even for women who are not consciously aware of sexual responses. Some women report, or their husbands' observe, that even though vaginal lubrication and nipple erection—the physical manifestations of arousal in women—are happening during sexual play, they are not feeling aroused.

This gap between physical manifestations of arousal and feelings of arousal exists because women function on two tracks—the physical and the emotional. These two tracks have to be in sync for you to experience the arousal responses. In other words, women must feel emotionally connected and cherished *and* be aware of their bodies to feel aroused. In contrast, men typically function on one track; when they are physically responding they feel aroused.

Which is true for you? Discuss this with your husband.

Listen to Your Body by Knowing Your Sexual Triggers

A woman's entire body can experience sexual feelings and responses. It is important to know and understand those areas of your body that are particularly sensitive to sexual impulses, feelings, and stimulation.

Some women are highly responsive to kisses on the neck, while others find such kisses too intense. Still others have no particular response whatsoever to neck kisses. The same can be true of stimulation around the ears. Stroking the inner thighs from above the knees to the genitals can help women be more receptive to genital touching, and can even bring heightened arousal and orgasm for some. The best place to start might be the feet. Studies about sex and the brain[3] have indicated that women are more likely to orgasm when their feet are warm, so you might use that fact to get foot massages from your husband.

Typically, the most sexually sensitive areas are the lips, breasts, clitoris, and vagina. Lips and mouth are intense areas of sexual responsiveness. Lip and tongue contact usually stirs up feelings in the genital area. The same is true of breast stimulation for many women.

Some women tend to resist passionate kissing and breast stimulation, even though they wish for the genital responsiveness. These women may struggle with an internal ambivalence about sexual responsiveness—they want the result, but resist the feelings. Since there are many variations from one woman to another as well as in a particular woman from one time to another, it is vital that you pay close attention to what is true for you and share that with your husband.

Equally important for you is to understand your genital area. Most women respond to clitoral external stimulation. When a woman becomes aroused, the lower third of the vagina engorges to form the orgasmic platform for sexual arousal and response, while the remaining upper portion balloons out to form the seminal pool, which receives and holds the man's ejaculate so she can more easily become pregnant. This shows how a woman's body is designed for both sexual pleasure and for procreation.

Whether we're talking about the neck, lips, breasts, ears, or genitals—and all the way down to the toes—every part of the body can be a source of pleasure. So be aware of what is true for you. Try not to impose onto yourself someone else's experience. The intensity of your response, positive or negative, can be determined only by you, so that's why you must listen to your body.

Listen to Your Body by Knowing Your Brain

Research on sex and the brain[4] has affirmed our years of clinical observation of women and their sexuality, as well as added new understandings. Our brains can work for us or against us sexually. The messages we received about sex growing up may have led to eager, positive anticipation of sex in marriage or might have filled us with apprehension and aversion.

Our observation is that sexual responses are easily conditioned early in life—and self-perpetuating unless intentionally countered.

You are fortunate if your early experiences and messages were positive. If those experiences were negative or created patterns not conducive to mutually fulfilling sex in marriage, you will likely need to work with a qualified sex therapist or pursue self-help to undo past negative influences and build positive experiences. That will take education, communication, and relearning the physical sexual process. The good news is that this process can lead to pleasure.

Relearning begins by receiving pleasurable caresses that start far from genitals—on the feet, for instance. This activity removes any expectations of sexual arousal and release—there's no pressure. The brain needs to be reprogrammed step-by-step; your current sexual experiences are ruled out, and you start over by retraining your body to respond as it was designed to respond.[5]

If your experiences were negative, you may feel stuck and hopeless now, but even as sexual responses can be conditioned, they can be reconditioned.

Maggie had her first orgasmic response when she was babysitting and happened upon pornography. Now in marriage, she can experience orgasm only if she visualizes women's breasts and genitals (the stimulus for that first response). Other women have learned to respond in a way that doesn't work with a man. In both situations, women can retrain their bodies to respond to their husbands through the step-by-step program we and others offer.

Women can retrain their bodies to respond to their husbands.

The female brain is more complex sexually than the male brain; it is also much less predictable and is ever changing. In *The Female Brain*, Louann Brizendine writes: "In all menstruating women, the female brain changes a little every day. Some parts of the brain change up to 25 percent every month. Things get pretty rocky at times. . . . If a woman's reality could change radically from week to week, the same would have to be true of the massive hormonal changes that occur throughout a woman's life."[6]

What goes on in the brain of a woman during a sexual experience is very complicated. Barry Komisaruk and his research group from Rutgers University found that different brain regions in a woman were activated depending on which body part was being stimulated.[7]

You might ask, "What difference does that make to me?" When a woman is touched, the touch activates different regions of the brain as she moves from stimulation to orgasm. Because of this, it's important to explore with your husband how touch feels on various parts of your body. As you become aware of how different parts of your body respond when being stimulated, you can help your body move from stimulation to response.

Listen to Your Body by Knowing Your Hormones

All the effort in the world won't help if your hormones are out of balance. Since hormonal balance is a prerequisite to healthy sexual functioning, you'll need to attend to and take responsibility for your hormonal fluctuations. That's not always an easy task. You will need to find a physician who is open to evaluating your hormonal levels and guiding you in how best to balance them.

Premenstrual syndrome (PMS) can wreak havoc on tranquility for many; this may be a struggle for you. Do get help. Supplements can provide some relief. It is important to get at least 50 mg of vitamin B_6 per day and 400 mg of magnesium. You may find a PMS vitamin/mineral supplement that works well for you. Sometimes prescription medication is necessary.

Hormonal birth control now includes higher levels of progestin, which messes with sexual desire and sexual responsiveness. The increased progestin also can make the vagina more sensitive to pain.

> Your physiology can affect how you feel about sex.

Pregnancy, postpartum,[8] and *breast-feeding* hormonal changes can also affect women's sexual functioning. However, hormonal treatment would not be the solution since hormones given to the mother would affect the fetus during pregnancy and the infant who is breast-feeding. An eating plan (see Appendix 1) and a prenatal supplement can help.

Menopause[9] means a drop in estrogen and progesterone production, which causes thinning of the vaginal wall and decreased lubrication. Hormonal replacement is available, but frequently not encouraged due to concern about health risks.[10] For women who still have their ovaries, testosterone production may continue well past menopause. If testosterone lessens, so will sexual drive. A testosterone patch, cream, or pellets can be very helpful, but they require a physician's prescription.

Neurochemicals and hormones—your physiology—can greatly affect how you feel about sex and how you respond sexually.

Listen to Your Body by Knowing Your Potential

Once you know your body, have a sense of the female brain, and have the confidence that your hormones are working for you in the best way possible, you will be able to maximize your potential for sexual enjoyment.

Physically, be mindful of what you eat; engage in a minimum of twenty minutes of exercise per day;[11] get a healthy balance of sleep, rest, and life-invigorating activity; and freely pamper yourself once a week. All of these will contribute to your sexual potential. For a healthy eating plan that enhances hormonal balance, see Appendix 1.

Who you are sexually is influenced by what's true about you in general. Do you exercise regularly and keep your body in shape? Do you eat healthily or do you struggle with eating too much, not eating enough, or not eating a good balance of healthy foods? Do you tend to go to bed at 3 a.m. and get up at 6 a.m. so you're always exhausted? Your lifestyle choices have an impact on your sexual life.

How might you carve out restorative time for yourself and your marriage? If you are willing to pamper yourself, you will be more receptive to feeling sexual impulses and more responsive to your husband's initiation. Many women find themselves so exhausted from family, household, and career duties that they have no energy left over for their sexual life, a situation that hinders them, their spouse, and their relationship in general.

Design time in your life to pamper your body: This could mean taking a bubble bath, getting a massage, having your nails or hair done, or doing whatever it is that is recuperative for you. As you pamper yourself, take time to develop your inner ear and listen to your body's whispers. Feed those little impulses to help them grow.

Mentally, nurture positive anticipation of sexual times with your husband. In the middle of your busy day, take a few minutes to think about a hug or a kiss from him. Make sure to resolve conflicts that interfere with your desire to connect sexually, and take note of what helps you feel loved, close, and connected. Being in that closely connected state will enhance your sexual response.

Spiritually, watch that you don't fall into the trap of believing that sex is a biblical duty rather than an expression of deep spiritual maturity and awareness. Since our sexuality is God's design for us, as we grow spiritually, we have the potential to grow sexually. Hence, the more spiritual, the more sexual.[12] Go for it!

As you learn to listen to your body, your enjoyment of sex will grow. And you'll be ready for the next step toward embracing your God-given sexuality in marriage—leading.

CHAPTER 3

LEAD

SEX WORKS BEST when the woman leads with her sexuality, not with demand or control.

Jeannie wanted sex more often than her husband did and was frustrated with his lack of initiation. Rather than "leading with her sexuality," she complained and tried to get him to have sex with her by making threats. Her complaints and threats pushed him away; they were demands rather than invitations.

In contrast, Shari used her higher sexual drive to invite and lead. Jim tended to go to bed earlier than Shari because of his demanding life situation. Shari realized that he didn't often have the energy for sex that she had; she didn't take personally their difference in how often they desired sex.

Rather, she decided to go to bed with him, give him a back massage, snuggle up to him, and gently kiss and sometimes even playfully caress his genitals. Sometimes that activity led to a sexual experience; other times it was just a playful, connecting time. Either way, she was using her sexuality to lead and not demand.

To lead sexually may be a totally new concept for you. In many cultures, the man is expected to be the sexual leader. Isn't the wife supposed to submit to her husband? Isn't she supposed to meet his sexual needs?

Ephesians 5, in the *New American Standard Bible*, begins with, "Therefore be imitators of God, as beloved children; and walk in love, just as Christ also loved you, and gave Himself up for us, an offering and a sacrifice to God as a fragrant aroma." Verses 20 and 21 continue to tell us how we are to be "always giving thanks for all things in the name of our Lord Jesus Christ to God, even the Father; and be subject to one another in the fear of Christ." In verse 22 and on, the text explains how the wife is to be to the husband as the church is to Christ, and that the husband is to be to the wife as Christ is to the church, giving Himself up for the church.

Then Paul in verse 31 quotes the expectation for sexual union between a husband and wife as given in Genesis 2:24: "For this reason a man shall leave his father and his mother, and be joined to his wife; and they shall become one flesh." He continues in Ephesians 5:32 to explain that sexual union between husband and wife is the model of Christ and the church: "This mystery is great; but I am speaking with reference to Christ and the church."

Following this model is what we have found leads to a mutually fulfilling sex life in marriage, and it is the model of the sexual relationship between a husband and wife as is described in the Song of Solomon. It is what works because:

A turned-on woman is usually a turn-on to a man;
but a turned-on man can be a demand or pressure to a woman.

To Lead, Accept Intense Sexuality

Women are created to be intensely sexual. Even though men—during their peak years—produce higher levels of testosterone than women do, women produce this sex-drive hormone and are also wired to desire sex. Yes, a woman's drive is more complex than a man's; her emotions need to be connected with her body. Just because her body is responding doesn't mean she feels aroused; her responses are internal, and the hormones that fuel her responses vary throughout the month and throughout her life. Yet this sexual complexity doesn't mean women weren't made to have strong desire.

> Women are wired to desire sex.

A woman's intense sexuality is affirmed by Scripture: Right from the beginning, Genesis teaches that both male and female were created in the image of God. The Song of Solomon most clearly demonstrates that it is the woman who pursues her husband sexually, as you can see in the *New American Standard Bible*:

> May he kiss me with the kisses of his mouth! For your love is better than wine. (1:2)

> My beloved is to me a pouch of myrrh which lies all night between my breasts. (1:13)

> My beloved is mine, and I am his. (2:16)

> On my bed night after night I sought him whom my soul loves. (3:1)

At the end of Chapter 4 after fifteen verses of him proclaiming his adoration of her, she says,

> May my beloved come into his garden and eat its choice fruits! (4:16)

> I was asleep but my heart was awake. . . . My beloved was knocking. (5:2)

I arose to open to my beloved; and my hands dripped with myrrh, and my fingers with liquid myrrh. (5:5)

His mouth is full of sweetness. And he is wholly desirable. (5:16)

Come, my beloved, let us go out into the country. Let us spend the night in the villages. Let us rise early and go to the vineyards; let us see whether the vine has budded and its blossoms have opened, and whether the pomegranates have bloomed. There I will give you my love. (7:11-12)

First Corinthians 7:1-3 expresses sexual intensity most clearly in the Bible paraphrase *The Message*. Paul is answering the question of the church at Corinth: "Is it a good thing to have sexual relations? Certainly—but only within a certain context. It's good for a man to have a wife, and for a woman to have a husband. Sexual drives are strong, but marriage is strong enough to contain them and provide for a balanced and fulfilling sexual life in a world of sexual disorder."

A woman's sexuality is affirmed by God's design.

This passage doesn't say that the man is the one with the sexual need that his wife is to understand and fulfill. That teaching just isn't valid and doesn't work in the long term within a marriage; it doesn't leave either the man or the woman satisfied. Sexual drive is strong for both men and women. That is how God designed us!

A woman's intense sexuality is affirmed by how God designed her body: The clitoris is a woman's only body part with no other purpose than to receive and transmit sexual stimulation. For many women, stimulation of the clitoris is the most vital source of arousal and orgasmic response; for others, clitoral stimulation is the precursor to what they will experience later.

Think of the clitoris as a tiny penis. Even as men prefer the shaft of the penis to be stroked, women find that stroking along the labia, the clitoral shaft rather than the tip of the clitoris, is much more enjoyable. Experiment with how and where you like clitoral stimulation—on the head, the shaft, or the hood. Do you prefer a direct touch versus a broad-handed touch? What you like early in the sexual experience may differ compared with what you like later. Early in the experience, direct touch on the clitoris may be too intense. As a woman moves closer to orgasm, the clitoris retracts under the hood, which means she may tolerate, even need, more direct clitoral stimulation. Share this factoid with your husband, and then guide him during the sexual experience according to what your body wants at any given point.

Even though the clitoris is the primary source of stimulation for most women, the vagina is not only the receptor of the penis, but it is also sensitive to stimulation in some areas. The opening of the vagina may be what is particularly arousing for you, or it may be that you much prefer the stimulation of the lower third of the inside of the vagina—about two inches.

The lower or outer third is the area of the vagina controlled by the pubococcygeus (PC) or Kegel muscle.[1] This area swells and becomes the orgasmic platform as arousal builds. At the upper edge of the PC muscle on the front wall of the vagina is the G-spot area (Gräfenberg spot).[2] For some women, once they are aroused, stimulation of that area increases the intensity of the arousal, and may nudge them over the hill to a very intense orgasm that may include a release of fluid called female ejaculation or flooding.

Women who have not been educated on this possible response may stop their orgasm because it feels like they're going to wet the bed. The fluid released is not urine, but it does come out of the urethra. If you think this might be true for you, talk with your husband about the possibility, empty your bladder before sex, protect the bed, and then let it go. You both will likely enjoy the intense response.

You might be thinking, *If God designed me to be intensely sexual, why don't I experience sexual desire and responsiveness?* Even as all of mankind is designed to desire oneness with God and sin has interrupted that felt urge for many, sexual intensity and desire may have been blocked by past experience, antisexual teaching, sexual pain, or physical imbalance in the body.

To be the fully sexual person that you were created to be, you will need to affirm that you were made for and can expect sexual enjoyment and sexual release. The subtle or overt belief that sex is primarily for your husband will never lead to a full life of sexual satisfaction.

Rather, claim the fact deep down that you have as much possibility and responsibility to enjoy the sexual experience as does your husband. It has to be as good for you as it is for him if it is going to be good for both of you throughout your lifetime.

To Lead, Know Your Conditions

Knowing and communicating the conditions that make sex best for each of you will make sex better for both of you.

Think through and talk with your husband about the times sex has been best for you. What were the contributing factors? What made the difference? Was it the time of day, the location, how rested you were, how you were feeling about yourself or about him, the lack of outside pressures, or other factors?

Don't attempt to replicate the experience, but rather provide the best conditions. Trying to repeat a previous experience can lead to performance pressure, while considering the conditions usually makes way for a relaxing setting that will enhance your experience.

Every woman has certain needs. When those are met, she will tend to be open to a time of sexual connection and more likely to experience sexual fulfillment, gratification, and satisfaction. What are you aware that you need so you are ready? What conditions would increase your openness and responsiveness sexually?

It could be that you need the bedroom clean. You may do better after a time of sharing and conversation with your husband. It could be that once the kids are asleep, you enjoy having time to get at peace with your body. It could be that what does it for you is a message of thoughtfulness from your husband—a rose picked on the way in from his car, a call to see if he can pick up dinner so you don't have to cook, or his checking to see what you need from him.

Identify and share anything that contributes positively to your openness and enjoyment of sex with your husband. That's why we say you need to be clear within yourself and both of you should communicate and take responsibility to create your ideal conditions.

That balance of communicating and taking responsibility is so important. Women can tend to measure their spouse's love by his memory of their needs. Men's memories aren't always as good as women wish they were. Also, since you are the one with the need, you will feel it and, therefore, remember. Texting him a reminder of your need would be a huge benefit to both of you. For example, you might text him saying, "Can't wait to play with you tonight! Can you help the kids with their homework while I take a bath and prepare?"

To Lead, Pursue Sexual Pleasure

Since both Scripture and physiology affirm women's design for sexual pleasure and release, we counter the teaching or implication that sex is a man's need, and the woman's job is to fulfill his needs. Every New Testament teaching about sex in marriage incorporates an expectation for mutuality. The most direct teaching is expressed so well in 1 Corinthians 7:3-5 in *The Message*: "The marriage bed must be a place of mutuality —the husband seeking to satisfy his wife, the wife seeking to satisfy her husband. Marriage is not a place to 'stand up for your rights.' Marriage is a decision to serve the other, whether in bed or out."

To Lead, Express Your Likes and Dislikes in a Positive Way

Discover with your husband what it is that brings you pleasure. Communicate what it is your body is telling you.

We recommend using the Non-Demand Teaching (NDT) exercise that is part of the sexual retraining process in our book *Restoring the Pleasure*. You will also find it in Appendix 2B. Couples find the NDT is a comfortable process to use somewhat regularly to keep discovering and teaching each other about likes and dislikes.

Women particularly benefit from this exercise because of their complexity and tendency to change based on their monthly hormonal variations and life-stage hormonal changes. It's a great way to restart your sexual life after having a baby.

There is no way a husband can know and meet the complex and diverse sexual needs of his wife unless she guides him.

Sex will never be great if a woman expects her husband to automatically know how, where, and when she wants to be touched. It is like having an itch on your back where you can't reach; you need to be very specific about exactly how and where the other person should scratch.

Sexually, women have more complex body parts and responses than men do. Because of women's complexity and tendency to change from one experience to another, telling your husband once about your likes and dislikes is not enough. It works much better for you to take responsibility for what you like and tell him or guide him in the moment.

We have had so many couples come to us for help, the wife complaining that her husband doesn't love her or doesn't really care because she has told him what she likes and he isn't doing it. As we listen to both of them, it becomes clear that he is not intentionally neglecting what she has told him; he really doesn't remember or thinks he is doing what she said. As we empower the wife to go after what she would like and guide him or direct him in the moment, both end up so relieved and happy.

Carrie had been frustrated with Jerry most of their three years of married life. On their honeymoon, Jerry had stimulated her too directly on her clitoris, which was more painful than pleasurable. She told him and thought he understood, but she had not discussed the issue since then. By the time they came to our office, her frustration was high and his feeling of sexual adequacy had dwindled radically. They had both concluded that they were sexually incompatible.

In reviewing the data we gathered from them both, it seemed too simple that the issue of how he touched her genitally could be the main issue behind their despair, but we decided to pursue that possibility. We assigned them the Clinical Genital Exam (part of our sexual retraining in *Restoring the Pleasure* and available in Appendix 2A), as well as the Non-Demand Teaching exercise (also part of our sexual retraining process in *Restoring the Pleasure* and available in Appendix 2B).

To their surprise and our encouragement, they resolved the issue that had led them to years of conflict and discouragement.

Resolution of sexual issues is usually not simple, but many times lack of communication and false expectations can get in the way of what could be a delightful and mutually fulfilling sexual life. When a woman learns to lead, she can lovingly inform her husband of how, where, and to what intensity she would like to be touched. This type of leading is a dominant factor in finding joy and mutual fulfillment.

CHAPTER 4

PLAN AND PREPARE

GOOD SEX in marriage doesn't just happen. Couples who keep the sexual spark glowing through the stages of marriage are those who are intentional about their sexual relationship. That's why we encourage you to plan for your times together rather than wait for spontaneity. We are convinced that:

> The anticipation of planned times
> increases the quality of those times, and the allotment of
> time together increases the quantity of lovemaking.

Consider a special time you marked on your calendar: Maybe it was a celebration of a birthday or going on a date or having a party. When you set a date and planned for the special event, you had time to get yourself ready—to prepare both physically and mentally. You may have had moments of anxiety, wondering if the upcoming event would turn out as you anticipated, and you likely felt excited as you looked forward to it.

The same can be true if you schedule a time to be together sexually. Yet many hold on to the notion that sex must be spontaneous. If spontaneity is working for you sexually, go for it. But we have found that the very couples who insist on spontaneity are those who are not happy with the frequency or the quality of their sexual times together.

Planning doesn't mean that every sexual time together needs to be a special event. Spontaneous quickies can be fun, delightful, and even satisfying if they aren't the consistent diet. While a person could survive on McDonald's meals, most of us enjoy an occasional "gourmet delight" and regular old-fashioned, healthy, home-cooked meals. Similarly, taking time to plan a sexual gourmet event and regular, basic, comfortable, homey sex times will bring deeper intimacy and passion for both of you.

Gourmet Plans

When you plan a special "gourmet" time, think of what you both would enjoy. One of you insisting on your own agenda might place demand or pressure on the other. Plan this event as you would plan other special events for the two of you. Plan the activities, the setting, and the accoutrements.

For example, you might want to make sure the bedroom is clean, scented candles are lighted, and music you have enjoyed together is playing in the background. Prepare your bodies. Be sure teeth are brushed and flossed. You might start by showering together. Satin sheets can be a fun addition. A makeup brush to pleasure each other can be used to increase sensuous awareness. There are endless options.

Regular Plans

A good old-fashioned, at-home sexual time will include the basics of getting to know each other through touch, talk, and teaching. Start with a time of sharing with each other what some of your favorite sexual times include.

Move from that time of talking to teaching each other. Have one of you sit in front of the other, guiding the other's hands and communicating as you discover the touch that is most enjoyable (see Appendix 2). You can then delight in an extended time of taking turns caressing each other's total bodies, starting on the back and moving to the front when both of you are ready.

End with the relaxation resulting from the touching, or you might decide to complete the sex act. As long as progressing to sex doesn't feel like a demand to either of you, feel free, but don't make it an expectation of your planned times together and be sure it is a mutual decision.

A Fabulous Formula

Years ago, based on our observations of what was lacking for couples who came to us for sexual therapy and what brought mutual sexual satisfaction into their lives, we created our "Formula for Intimacy." Later, research about sex and the brain affirmed why this formula of daily hugs, kisses, and emotional and spiritual connection had a positive impact on couples' sexual satisfaction.

Looking into each other's eyes and hugging has been shown to release oxytocin,[1] a brain chemical associated with bonding. Kissing stimulates nerve endings on our lips, which sparks the release of dopamine. Dopamine is a neurotransmitter that is active in circuits in the brain associated with pleasure and reward, which means kissing can lead you to wanting more.

The fifteen minutes per day of connecting prescribed by our Formula for Intimacy includes eye-to-eye contact and a twenty-second hug to release the oxytocin, as well as the five- to thirty-second passionate kiss to stimulate a bit of dopamine spark.

We strongly encourage you to make a weekly time commitment for your marriage's sexual intimacy. The benefits for couples are similar to the benefits for individuals who practice disciplines to grow in their relationship with God.

When a relationship with God is new, natural enthusiasm motivates desire to spend time with Him. But over time, we realize that we need intentional structure—time set aside to be with God—to grow and flourish spiritually. Likewise, to grow in intimacy in marriage, it will take the discipline of manageable time commitments.

If you take one positive step toward intentional connecting, we recommend you practice our Formula for Intimacy.[2] The most important part of the formula is the prescription for fifteen minutes of connecting emotionally, spiritually, and physically every day.

Follow it as you would medical advice, exactly in the order indicated, with the emotional connecting time coming first. You might want to buy a fifteen-minute sand timer to keep track of the time. Another idea is to use a devotional book or flip calendar for couples to encourage spiritual connection.

Formula for Intimacy

15 MINUTES A DAY TO:
- **connect emotionally:** look into each other's eyes (↑ oxytocin: trust hormone); share a positive thought, feeling, and/or affirmation of the other.
- **connect spiritually:** share an inspirational reading and prayer.
- **connect physically:** hug for 20 seconds (↑ oxytocin); kiss passionately for 5–30 seconds without leading to sex (↑ dopamine: passion hormone).

ONE EVENING A WEEK: walk, date, shower, caress, no demands

ONE DAY A QUARTER: fun, play, lead and teach enjoyable touch

ONE WEEKEND A YEAR: together away or at home, no distractions

Penner & Penner
www.passionatecommitment.com

The next important component of our formula is your weekly time for connection. Decide together if you prefer to set a specific day and time for each week, or if you prefer to decide the day week by week. If you vary the day there is more risk of missing it, so commit to a time to choose the day.

You might schedule Sunday evening to look at your calendars and choose the day and time for the upcoming week. Decide together who will ensure that this meeting happens, and then during the meeting, agree about how you plan to use your weekly connection time.

If you have children, you will need to determine how you will manage them during your private time. You may have to be creative. Be sure to start your weekly time together at least an hour before you want to be asleep.

The quarterly day of connection and the yearly weekend are special times that will require additional planning. Just be sure you are realistic in your plans.

In addition to our observations and the brain research that explains why our recommendations for connecting actually make a positive difference, a study showed that scheduling sexual times helped women synchronize their sexual desire with that of their male partner. The study also indicated a boost in couples' sexual satisfaction as a result of pre-planning. Meeting once a week for sexual connection was ideal for the maximum benefits. More than weekly wasn't necessarily better.[3]

> Planning ahead can lead you to greater enjoyment and more intimacy.

So don't believe the myth that "scheduling" your sex life is boring! As you can see from our counseling experiences and from other studies, the opposite is true. Planning ahead can lead you to great enjoyment and more intimacy with your husband.

Prepare

As you plan for your sexual times together, you can also prepare for the best conditions during that time. Consider this as another step in anticipation of your special time together.

While sex with your husband will rarely be a "ten" because of the distractions of children, the energy drain of life, illness, relationship stress, and many other interruptions, you *can* create the best possible conditions given your situation and phase of life.

To make your time together the best it can be at the moment, consider the atmosphere and your attitude while also cultivating affection between the two of you.

Charles and Connie had started their marriage with sexual enthusiasm and a lot of fun and fulfillment for both of them. But because she needed to take an antibiotic and wasn't aware that it could interfere with the effectiveness of her hormonal birth control, she became pregnant within the first six months of their marriage.

Nausea during pregnancy and adjustment to being parents interfered with the enjoyment they had experienced in those early months before pregnancy. They e-mailed us for help.

We suggested they do the following:

TALK TOGETHER AND JOT DOWN . . .

- When have you had your best times?

- What contributed to those times being better than other times?

- What is the best time of day for the two of you? Is it the morning or the evening? If one of you prefers morning and the other evening, maybe you can sneak home for a "nooner" or negotiate alternating morning times and evening times.

- How has the baby's (or children's) schedule affected your sexual times, and how might you work around or adapt that schedule?

- As you talk about when you have had your best times and what contributed to those, share the factors that were most important to each of you, and try to incorporate both of your perspectives.

Charles and Connie e-mailed back a detailed response to our suggestions. As they considered our suggestions, they realized that they had expected sex to just happen as it had before the pregnancy and childbirth.

They decided to make a few changes in the baby's schedule and to plan for their times together. For them, it worked best to make a specific plan each week rather than a standard weekly plan. His work schedule was variable, so when he knew what the next week was going to entail, they planned to sit down together and decide on their sexual times for the week ahead.

This gave Connie time to think about and positively anticipate their planned rendezvous. She was able to give herself fully to the baby beforehand, which made it easier for her to shift to their time together. The baby was more content and she felt freer to enjoy herself sexually.

Women seem to respond more and be more affected than men—both positively and negatively—to various factors surrounding a sexual experience. Because of this, knowing and communicating the conditions that make sex best for you will make sex better for both of you.

There is no way your husband can know and prepare for, respond to, or respect your complex needs unless you inform him and also do your part to make sure those requirements are met.

As you prepare for your sexual times together, incorporate what you have learned as you discussed the previous bulleted questions. You might create a checklist together that you can refer to each time. Some requirements on the list may be higher priorities than others. Over time, you will likely discover new criteria and ideas to add to your list and, possibly, scratch others from your list.

As you make your list and prepare for your sexual times together, you'll need to consider your privacy, the atmosphere, your attitude, and your affection for each other.

Ensure Privacy

Do attend to some commonsense practical solutions to counter interruptions and increase the passion and intimacy of your married sexual relationship.

- Put a lock on your bedroom door, and use that lock every time you engage in sexual play of any kind.

- Turn off the ringer phones and cell phones or put all phones and electronic devices out of the room.

- Pets also need to be out of the room and contained where they can't be scratching or calling at the door.

- Children are a little more difficult to manage, but be creative so that for your good and theirs, you maintain privacy.

- Bring to the location anything you might want to use during your sexual time: lubricant, contraceptive, washcloth.

Create the Atmosphere

What settings do you both enjoy most or find are most conducive to a positive encounter?

You might decide you have the best times when you are away from home at a hotel or other setting. Since that requirement may not be financially or practically realistic, you can choose those ideal settings for your quarterly or yearly times of practicing our Formula for Intimacy.

Whatever the setting, vary it if possible. It is easy to resort to your bed and bedroom—and that may be your only option. If you have the house to yourselves, choose another room some of the time. If you have only one appropriate space to be together sexually, vary where and how you use that space. Let's say it is your bedroom. You might put a comforter on the floor or change your location on the bed so your heads are at the side or the foot end of the bed.

Within the setting, prepare your environment. If it is important for either or both of you to have a space that is organized, prepare that ahead of time. Decide if you will clean up together, take turns, or if one of you will do that task. Do candles or music or scent help you relax or get in touch with your body or with each other? Do you like the room light, dark, or dimly lit? What kind of surface feels best on your skin? Cotton, flannel, satin, silky, fuzzy, or other? You might find a throw blanket in that texture that you can put down where you will be enjoying your time together.

Adjust Your Attitude

Prepare yourself mentally for your sexual times together. If your times are planned, you will have time to think about and visualize positive sexual interaction and then create that affirmative attitude and approach. To prepare yourself physically, also get in touch with your body and any internal sexual sensations. Practice the listening we discussed in Chapter 2.

Prepare yourself throughout the day.

Prepare yourself throughout the day by thinking about what you both enjoy. Create and encourage a sense of fun and mutual enjoyment.

What else do you need to enhance your positive anticipation of sex with your husband? It might be best if you had a power nap that day. Or maybe you feel best when you've taken a bubble bath, showered, or shaved your legs. What you need to support your positive attitude is unique. Don't keep those needs a secret. Do it!

Include Affection

What kind of affection and connection do you need to be ready to open up sexually? Get to know yourself and take responsibility to create the opportunity for what you need. Instead of focusing on what your spouse could do to make sex better, do what you can do to make it good for you! If you make it good for you, it will likely be good for him.

Now that you know more about planning and preparing for sexual times with your husband, it's time to focus on pleasure.

CHAPTER 5

PLEASURE

Focus on pleasure rather than response. Passion in marriage will last only if the focus is on pleasurable touch—not on the goal of arousal, orgasm, or intercourse.

Yet it can be difficult to learn to enjoy the journey rather than pursue the goal. Orgasm is often seen as the ultimate measure of sexual success. So, many come to us desperate because they have not been able to "achieve" orgasm.

Since the orgasmic response is an involuntary reflex that is triggered when we are freely enjoying ourselves, getting adequate stimulation, and not watching whether it is "working," setting orgasm as the goal actually interferes with that possibility.

It is so natural to want that response. And when it hasn't come easily, it's also easy to become focused on *trying* rather than on the enjoyment of the touch and the intensity of the good feelings.

When we talk about pleasuring, we are talking about giving and receiving touch in a way that is pleasant, relaxing, and feels nice to both spouses. You can learn to give and receive touch in a way that feels good to you and is positive for your husband.

How might you learn to take in touch and experience pleasure if that has not been an option or reality for you? You might start with learning to enjoy a warm bubble bath, or putting lotion on your body, or making an appointment for a therapeutic body massage or foot reflexology session—whatever pampering or nonsexual caress helps you soak in the sensation of touch.

After you learn to enjoy touch for your own body, you and your husband might take turns learning to give and receive touch.

New patterns of physical relating will be established as you each develop awareness of your own sensations and take responsibility to pursue your desires and communicate your needs, *but not at the expense of the other*.

Take time to learn about your own and each other's bodies and about the type of touch you most enjoy. Openly communicate about yourselves and your sexual experience. If talking about sex doesn't come easily, we find reading a book about sex aloud together can break barriers and provide the structure and tools you need to talk more freely. You may choose to read this book or another out loud together.

Take time to learn about each other's bodies.

You might start learning to give and receive touch by giving each other a foot caress. If that goes well, try taking turns with giving back caresses. You might progress to total body caressing, but not including breast or genital stimulation.

Then add some more creative experiences, such as using any other part of your bodies, except your hands, to pleasure each other. Or you could have fun selecting objects of varying textures to try on the other's back. See if each of you can guess what the objects are and then choose which you would like your spouse to use to pleasure your entire body.

As you begin to experiment with touch, familiarize yourself with the process of learning to soak in touch as both the *receiver* and *pleasurer*.

Receiving and Caressing: As both pleasurer and receiver, we must take responsibility for discovering, communicating, and going after our sexual feelings and desires, but not at the other's expense. Demand on our spouse is reduced when we can count on each other to share from within, rather than expecting the other to produce a response in us. We can give our bodies to each other to enjoy, but we cannot produce in each other the involuntary responses of arousal and release. Following this principle, there are "job descriptions" for the receiver and the pleasurer.

Receiver: Your only task is to soak in the touch and to redirect the pleasurer when the touch is not pleasing. Express your concern if at any time you start to wonder whether your spouse is not enjoying himself or herself.

Pleasurer: Your task is to lovingly touch your spouse in a way that feels good to you, enjoying his or her body for your pleasure. Think of radiating warmth though your fingertips (or any other part of your body) and taking in the sensation of warmth and the pulsation of your spouse's body. You might imagine that you are a blind person discovering your spouse through touch.

Encourage your spouse to redirect you if what you are doing is negative to him, and you do the same when he is pleasuring you. Express your concern if at any time you become anxious rather than enjoying your spouse's body. Caress *slowly*. Take time to mesh, relax, and discover the kind of touch that feels good to both of you.[1]

If you can really believe that your sexuality was designed for your pleasure and fulfillment, not just your husband's, then it will be easier for you to become comfortable in both giving and receiving touch. You will be able to focus on what is most fulfilling and pleasurable for you, even as you enjoy him and he enjoys you. As you learn to savor and enjoy the touch, you will both, inevitably, find great mutual fulfillment.

For more structured experiences in the giving and receiving of pleasure, the touching assignments in our book *Restoring the Pleasure*[2] provide opportunities for each of you to learn to enjoy each other's bodies for your own pleasure through touching, and to soak in the pleasure when you are being touched.

We teach four techniques to slow the pace and soak in the touch:

1. Touch in circles rather than straight lines.
2. Move your hands with the contour of your spouse's body rather than use a flat hand.
3. Keep his pace lagging slightly behind yours in both activity and intensity (in other words, you lead both in level of sexual activity and in the intensity of response).
4. Kiss passionately daily without it being an indicator of wanting sex or leading to sex.

Enjoy the Journey of Kissing

You'll hear the emphasis on kissing in all of our writing and speaking. We believe that the passionate connection of kissing is vital for a fulfilling sex life. So spend some time thinking about your history and present situation with kissing.

What kissing experiences did you have in your growing-up years? Was there kissing in your dating history before you met your husband? If so, what was that like for you? Did you enjoy kissing passionately? Or did you avoid it? Or maybe you did it but didn't like it?

What was your kissing history with your husband during dating and engagement? Was it passionate and enjoyable? If not, what was that about? If so, is that still true? If not, when did kissing change from positive to what it is now?

We find that kissing is the best indicator of how sex will be. If kissing is good, it's likely that sex is good. When a couple is able to passionately kiss and feel the connection between their lips and their genitals internally, typically sex is going well also. If you are both enjoying passionate kissing, you have a solid base for giving and receiving pleasure through touch.

When a woman isn't enjoying kissing, we've found there can be a number of reasons for this problem. It could be that she had uncomfortable sexual sensations stirred up with mouth-to-mouth kissing during childhood with a parent, grandparent, or other person. Or she may have had a negative experience in dating before she became connected with the person who is now her husband.

It may be that she never liked how her husband kissed, even in dating, but didn't deal with that disconnect. It may be that she felt he always led and was too aggressive in his kissing, or that the kissing was too slobbery.

It may be that kissing was passionate and enjoyable, but then she shut down on it to keep from going too far sexually before marriage. And now that she's married, she hasn't been able to turn it back on.

> If kissing is good, it's likely that sex is good.

Some women develop a common pattern of kissing passionately only when they want to have sex. If they are not sure they want to have sex, they don't kiss lest they "lead him on." This is why passionate kissing without leading to sex is assigned as part of our Formula for Intimacy (page 40).

Whatever was true for you before can be rectified now—and needs to be—if you are going to have an abundant life of sexual pleasure. If you are not having any or very little passionate kissing now, you can start over and learn what is most pleasurable to both of you. Kissing is vital for the ongoing sexual relationship.

Sarah and Jerry came to us after ten years of marriage and little sexual enjoyment. As we talked, Sarah shared that she had not enjoyed kissing Jerry since sometime before they married.

As we learned their history, we discovered that kissing had so aroused Sarah early on that they had stopped kissing passionately to avoid going too far before marriage. They both expected that once they were married and could have sex, all of that passion would return.

Yet after three years of shutting off those feelings in an effort to control their actions before marriage, neither kissing nor sex were enjoyable for Sarah. She kept waiting for the passion she had felt originally.

Eventually she was able to back up and gradually learn to lead in the kissing without expecting the initial feelings of their kissing in dating. Instead, she accepted the closeness, tenderness, and comfort, and then started to enjoy the intimacy of the kissing. As the warmth of intimate kissing grew, the sexual enjoyment increased as well.

Missy and Bill came to us for premarital counseling. Missy's difficulty with kissing was different; she had enjoyed kissing in other relationships, but didn't like how Bill kissed. Because she felt uncomfortable sharing this with Bill, they had never discussed it.

She was able to share this when we met with her alone. Then we were able to bring it up with them together. Both wanted to work on finding a way to kiss that was good for her. It was important for her to lead and teach him how she liked to kiss. She liked less use of the tongue and less saliva.

When he became aware of her likes and dislikes and she lead him, they were able to enjoy kissing. She felt such a relief and found she actually loved kissing more than she ever had.

If kissing isn't good for you, start by asking for a time when you can talk about it with your spouse. Follow the effective communication skills that you will find in the next chapter. Start with a statement about kissing that is an "I" statement, not a "you" statement. Here's an example: "I've been reading this book and have realized that kissing has never been good for me. I'd like to work on it." Then share what you have learned as you have read.

After that, you might suggest that the two of you experiment with kissing, with you leading and trying to get a sense of what might be good for you. Be sure not to expect that it will be warm and romantic, but more instructional and for the purpose of discovery and learning. You might add some fun. One couple used their tongues to pass a Life Saver candy back and forth between them.

You can also start practicing the daily fifteen-minute connecting time that ends with passionate kissing. Until kissing is positive for you, make sure you lead in the kissing and kiss for only as long as it remains positive. It may start with just warm lip-to-lip embrace for a few seconds, and then gradually increase in length and intensity. Once again, think of taking small steps as shown on the diagram on page 11.

One woman e-mailed us saying, "Thank you so, so much for your instruction on kissing. At the seminar, I told Roy for the first time that I had never enjoyed kissing. We determined to follow your guidance. It has been seven months of my gradually experimenting with what I like and don't like. When he starts to take over and kiss me, we have a fun signal I give him that lets him know to stick with my level of involvement and intensity. Kissing has become fun, and we've even had moments of my being free to engage in full-mouth, intense kissing. I have gotten over my concern as to what I will do if he gets aroused. I keep reminding myself that you said he gets aroused every eighty to ninety minutes while he sleeps and nothing has to be done about those responses, so just enjoy. And we do!!"

If you love passionate kissing, that is *great*! Enjoy it regularly. Pucker up—kiss, kiss, and keep kissing!

As you experiment with kissing and touch, remember to enjoy the journey of pleasure and release the focus on the "destination."

CHAPTER 6

TALK

TALKING ABOUT YOUR SEXUAL RELATIONSHIP with your husband is vital to keeping love, passion, and intimacy alive. Unfortunately, many couples haven't learned to share openly with each other about sex.

If you grew up in a home where sex wasn't talked about, you may have difficulty addressing sex topics. If you have tried talking and talking hasn't helped, you may have given up. Maybe every attempt to talk about your sex life has led to so much conflict that you've never felt heard or made progress.

Ultimately, the goal will be for you and your husband to get comfortable discussing all aspects of the sexual experience: your body anatomy, your arousal and response, what goes on inside of your body, what you are aware of emotionally, your likes and dislikes, and what you need to enjoy your full potential together sexually.

Jon and Melissa contacted us after five years of marriage and many unsuccessful attempts at discussing their sexual differences. Jon believed that if he understood his wife's view, he would be "giving in" to her. Melissa was convinced that Jon needed to see her side before she would be able to comprehend his view. Obviously, this was a tenacious impasse.

In this case, a third party (the two of us) was needed. We listened to each of their perspectives separately and clarified their viewpoints until each felt truly heard and understood. Following that, we met with them together. We told them we would start by presenting what we understood was Melissa's viewpoint, and have her affirm or correct us as we did so.

Then we asked Jon to look his wife in the eyes and tell her what he now understood were her concerns, making clear his understanding did not indicate agreement, only care and understanding. Tears ran down Melissa's cheeks as he spoke to her. She reached for his hand and thanked him.

Start by reading a book about sex aloud together.

After taking time to savor that new moment of realizing how his understanding affected both of them, Melissa was able to look Jon in the eyes and tell him what she understood as his perspective. Jon's issues were based on deeper early childhood trauma, so our involvement was necessary for him to feel heard by her.

If you have difficulty talking about your sexual life as a couple, you may need to seek the help of a therapist, but not always. So start by reading this or another book about sex aloud together. Two of our books that couples find helpful are *The Gift of Sex* and *The Married Guy's Guide to Great Sex*. Read a paragraph or short section and then discuss what you've read.

Make sure that you each share your reactions. First share your own reaction, and then have your husband repeat what he heard from you. After that, you should confirm or clarify your husband's response to ensure there are no misunderstandings. Your husband can then share his reaction, and you will follow the same process of listening and responding.

Before you begin talking, create a setting without distractions. Turn to each other, make eye contact, and take turns sharing and listening.

When you are the one sharing, follow these guidelines:

- Be aware of your emotions. Take some deep breaths and relax your body and mind as much as possible.

- Calm your voice.

- Avoid blame. Use "I" statements about what you think and feel, rather than "you" statements.

- Avoid generalizations. Don't use the words *always* and *never*.

When you are the listener, it's important to:

- Put aside your thoughts and focus completely on your husband and what he is sharing—his perspective.

- Listen without criticism, judgment, or interruption.

- Be aware of your own thoughts and reactions that might get in the way.

- Respond with expressions of care and without evaluation. Practice empathizing with him by reflecting what you have heard and sensed. You can say that you experience it differently but that you truly want to understand and accept how he views what you have sensed. It is okay to agree to disagree, but it's important to care about the other's perspective.

Here's our model for active listening and the specific steps for you to follow.

COMMUNICATION MODEL

MESSAGE SENT
Words, gestures, symbols, body language

FEEDBACK
What receiver heard and saw, including emotional aspects

CLARIFY
Any unclear feedback

Communication Format

For all communication, look into each other's eyes to increase the brain chemical oxytocin, which builds trust and attachment; actively listen; and share honestly and openly with no sense of judgment.[1]

Step 1

    A. Each should think through or write what you would like to share on the topic to be discussed.

    B. To determine what you think, feel, or need, write whatever comes to your mind.

    C. Read your responses aloud to yourselves first. Then carefully choose and write the words you want to use to communicate most clearly to your spouse. Share these responses with your spouse. Decide who will share first. Since the model has the man sending the message first, that is how it will be written in the steps below.

Step 2

A. While your husband is sharing, you are to put aside your thoughts and feelings about what he is sharing and about what you want to share on this topic.

B. To increase listening ability, position your bodies so that you are facing each other. You may hold hands, but *only if* that is not distracting for either of you. Look at each other. As the listener, watch his expressions, feelings, and body language, and listen carefully to his words.

C. Put into words what you heard him say and what you sensed he was feeling. You might try several different words to reflect your sense of what he communicated. Avoid labels, evaluations, or judgments.

Avoid:	Try This:
You make me the problem.	I sense you are affected by my . . . Say more about that.
That is always what you say.	I have heard that from you before, but let me make sure I understand you correctly.
That just isn't true.	So you experience . . .

Step 3

A. He needs to listen carefully to your reflection of his sharing. Continue to position yourselves so you have eye contact as you try to empathize with him and understand his perspective.

B. Your husband either affirms that he communicated accurately and was heard correctly, or he clarifies, rephrases, or adds to his first message. If his words and gestures did not communicate the first time, he will try new words to share his thoughts and feelings.

Step 3 was difficult for Jon. Jon had a distant, cold, punitive mother who was unable to empathize with him. With that deep trauma, he could not "hear" Melissa's care and empathy for him. Because of this, he needed therapeutic intervention.

Communication is complete when the message receiver has been able to put the message sender's words and feelings into the receiver's own words *and* the message sender has recognized the accuracy of the feedback. When you both agree that this process has been completed, reverse roles. The message sender will now be the receiver, and the message receiver will be the sender. Repeat steps 1, 2, and 3.

Go to http://www.wikihow.com/Actively-Listen for a helpful description of how to listen effectively and respond helpfully. Many couples are able to gain resolution through this process. But if you cannot, do seek outside help.

Topics to Discuss

God and Sex

Invite God into your sexual activities. Discuss any religious teaching or input you received about sex.

Your Ever-Changing Complexity

Since a woman is complex sexually and her responses vary, it is essential that you keep your husband informed about what's going on with you in your particular situation at all times. There is no way he can keep up and know where you are in your body and emotions from one day to the next. Taking responsibility for communicating how you feel and what will and won't work for you will greatly reduce his confusion and feelings of rejection. Such communication will also greatly reduce frustration for you, since you won't feel as misunderstood by him.

Adaptations Needed Because of Life Changes

MENSTRUAL CYCLE

If you are menstruating, keep track of your cycle, especially noting when in your cycle you experience higher or lower levels of sexual desire. Keep your husband informed. Day one of your cycle is the day you start bleeding. The "Follicular Phase" of your cycle is the time from the start of your period until you ovulate. Estradiol, one form of estrogen (what we often refer to as the "happy hormone"), builds to its peak right before ovulation. (Ovulation is the time when you release an egg and can become pregnant.)

The "Luteal Phase" of your cycle, when your body creates high amounts of the hormone progesterone, starts after ovulation and continues until right before you start your next period. This is when many women experience irritability, cravings, bloating, and other PMS symptoms. There are good vitamin/mineral supplements to help reduce those symptoms.

Keep your husband informed.

If you are interested in more detail related to your personal menstruation chart and the impact of your hormones on you, a great resource is *Taking Charge of Your Fertility* by Toni Weschler.[2] There are also several resources that can help you keep track of your cycle:

- Clue is a free app that makes it easy for women to find patterns in their cycle, from first period to menopause.

- MyMonthlyCycles.com is a website that offers free personalized tools to track your monthly menstrual cycles. Visit www.menstruation.com.au/periodpages/chartingcycles.html.

DURING PREGNANCY, AFTER CHILDBIRTH, AND DURING BREAST-FEEDING

At these times, women's bodies change significantly. Each woman is different and sometimes each pregnancy is different. It will take time to understand what is going on for you; it certainly will take communication with your husband for him to ride these changes with you. You will need to be kind and patient with yourself and with him.

THE YEARS WITH CHILDREN IN THE HOME

Having kids affects a couple's sex life significantly. If you didn't schedule sexual times for the two of you before you had children, you certainly will need to after your first child comes along.

MENOPAUSAL CHANGES

These changes usually start slowly and can be subtle—and therefore confusing. The changes that affect sex are the thinning of the vaginal wall, decreased vaginal lubrication, and vaginal atrophy.[3] You will experience less change if you continue to have sexual intercourse and exercise your pelvic floor muscles and/or enlist the help of a pelvic floor physical therapist.

Work out together how best to adapt.

As you are going through menopause and experiencing any of these life changes that affect you sexually, acknowledge your apprehensions and discomforts, but don't complain before, during, or after sex. Rather, set aside times to talk about it and work out together how best to adapt and make sex the best it can be, given the reality of your situation.

Your Likes and Dislikes

Like many women, you may wonder how to share your sexual likes and dislikes with your husband. It is often easier to address these sensitive issues when you have a questionnaire to complete and share with each other. You might answer these questions and then share them with each other using our communication format described earlier in this chapter.

How I View Our Sexual Experiences: My Likes and Dislikes

I rate my sexual satisfaction as _____ on a scale of 1 to 5.

My satisfaction would increase if I could _____

_____

I would like to contribute to our sex life by _____

_____

I estimate that we have sex about _____ times per _____

I would like to have sex _____ times per_____

I think you would like to have sex _____ times per _____

I think I initiate _____ percent of the time.

I think you initiate _____ percent of the time.

I would like to make the following changes in our initiation pattern:

_____

_____

The activities I enjoy most during our sexual times are: _____

_____

_____

_____

The activities I think you would enjoy that I don't are: _____

_____

_____

_____

Answering these questions separately and taking turns sharing your answers using our communication format gives you both a chance to express yourselves. Hopefully you also will feel that you've been listened to and understood. Remember, repeating and clarifying your spouse's message is not the same as *agreeing* with it. Agreement isn't necessary; the goals are to feel heard and understood, and to find a solution that works for both of you.

We've found in counseling that there are a few questions commonly asked by women concerning likes and dislikes. Here's some general guidance concerning two particular questions and how to talk to your husband about these topics.

Q: "What is a good way to communicate to my husband that I want him to do something different than he is doing with me during sex? How do I talk to him without making him feel inadequate?"

A: To let your husband know if you would like him to do something differently—and with *any* communication that might be confrontational—we recommend using the SET approach.

S for Support: Express how much you care for him; share the general positive aspects of your sex life and about him as a lover.

E for Empathy: Try to put into words what you think he is feeling or thinking about what you hope to share. For example, clitoral stimulation often needs to be corrected, so you might say, "I know when you are stimulating me genitally I get aroused, so it makes sense that you would keep doing that. It probably feels good to you and seems like it feels good to me."

T for the Truth: Then share your truth with warmth and without criticism. For example, you might say, "But the truth is, I would love it if you moved away to my inner thigh, and we spent some time kissing. Then it would be great if you went back to my genitals and maybe touched along the sides rather than directly on the head of the clitoris. But I know we may need to experiment with how I might guide you at the time, because I do change what feels good as I get more aroused."

Q: "My husband loves oral sex, but it grosses me out. Is there a way I can overcome my disgust?"

A: If your husband enjoys a sexual activity and you don't, start by letting him know what you assume. So you might say, "I assume from what I have heard from you that you would really like to engage in oral sex."

Then express your concern about that: "I feel badly that I don't enjoy oral sex. In fact, it is so negative for me that I actually can't do it. What I can do is _____." Or "It isn't negative for me; I just feel shy or uncomfortable doing it. I would be willing to learn and start with small steps. Maybe you could just give me a little momentary kiss/peck on my genitals and then I do the same on your penis."

Or you might have conditions such as, "I would need our genitals to be freshly washed and maybe we put something on them that is edible and tastes good."

After you share your thoughts, listen to his viewpoint. And then reflect his viewpoint and clarify it if necessary. Talk about it until you come to an agreement on how you will proceed.

Some men do make sexual activity requests that we believe are not healthy or do not meet biblical principles for sex in marriage. Three of these are anal sex, pornography use alone or together, and having others participate in sex with the two of you. As you learn to communicate about sex, it might be good to review these guiding principles concerning sexual activities in marriage.

GUIDING PRINCIPLES FOR RIGHT AND WRONG MARITAL SEXUAL ACTIVITIES

1. It must be an expression of love and not self-serving.

2. It must be mutual—as good for one as it is for the other.

3. The activity must draw you closer and build intimacy (biblically, sex is about "becoming one").

4. It doesn't interfere with your relationship with God or any biblical teaching.

5. Go with the most conservative spouse (in this case, the one who doesn't feel comfortable with oral sex), but that spouse must be willing to try to understand the needs and desires of the other.

In addition to sharing likes and dislikes, it's helpful to decide on prearranged signals that you and your husband might use during sex to invite touch, to change to a different body part, and to increase or decrease the intensity or firmness of the touch.

Use of a prearranged signal is particularly important for a woman who has suffered sexual trauma or if a sexual activity is particularly negative for her. For example, if you experience flashbacks of a violation, arrange with your husband that you will tap him on the shoulder or tug on his earlobe if a sexual activity is triggering you. That signal will let him know that you need him to change what he is doing.

Sometimes it's difficult for a woman to communicate what she likes because of her complexity. She might not really know what she likes until she is into the feelings of the experience. Communicating ways to signal during sex helps her husband enjoy her body and know what she likes. Both you and your husband will be more relaxed and free if you have talked about a way to address this.

If you're not sure what type of touch you will like on any given day, talk to your husband about guiding his hand to a part of your body that would feel good to you.

Keep talking, and even more important, keep listening. Enjoy!

CHAPTER 7

PRACTICE INTIMACY

Becoming one—sexual union in marriage—is a biblical expectation. It's not just performing a physical act. It's not just about getting a release. It's not about having needs met or meeting the other's needs. It's about true intimacy—connecting on all levels. *It is a human realization of a godly ideal.* Becoming one is achievable for all couples, but may take more work for some than for others.

Susan and Richard had grown up in the same church and in warm, healthy, nurturing homes. They had common friends and very similar values. But it wasn't until after college that they met again; they became reacquainted on a mission trip. Their friendship grew, and their romantic feelings became evident to them and everyone around them.

In contrast, Mary and Keith, who both came from troubled backgrounds, met after college in a single-adult church group. Both very attractive and socially desirable, they moved quickly into a romantic connection without much friendship development; sexual attraction and feelings were strong and fueled the growth of their relationship, rather than true intimacy.

Both couples waited for marriage to consummate their sexual relationship.

We met Susan and Richard while we were speaking at a couples' retreat. After six months of marriage, they had some questions about birth control and decisions regarding family planning. They seemed deeply connected; they looked into each other's eyes and moved closer as they shared their journey and delightful marital adjustment. We took the opportunity to ask them about their background and current experience as a married couple. Sex was great for both of them; they kissed passionately and both loved it. They truly enjoyed all aspects of married life.

Mary and Keith came to us for sexual therapy after six months of marriage. They were not having sex and were not kissing passionately. He felt awkward and distant; she felt frustrated and sexually needy.

Keith had been raised by a distant mother and had missed out on the bonding of infancy; Mary had been raised with a lot of warmth but also chaos, divorce, and neglect in her home. She began pushing for sex, and he began avoiding it. Their social life was great, and friends would assume they were doing well. But neither felt intimately connected.

Intimacy in marriage is worth working toward.

Our expectation of marriage is rather amazing: that two unique people, often from totally different backgrounds with differing assumptions and expectations, are to connect on a deep and intimate level and flow harmoniously together sexually "until death do us part."

One author and sex therapist addresses this expectation: "The more I learn about the nature of love and its expression through sexual intimacy, the more I am in awe of it. But sometimes I think we use the concept 'love is a mystery' to avoid the responsibility for the hard work true intimacy entails. We live in a culture in dire need of sexual education."[1]

Intimacy in marriage is worth working toward, however. Even as becoming one with God brings spiritual healing, becoming one in marriage has the potential to bring relational healing and relief from the anxiety that may come with being alone.

Let's look at what may keep intimacy from happening and how to pursue or increase connection in your marriage.

Obstacles to Intimacy

Fear

You may fear intimacy even if you long for it. The fear of intimacy is the fear of abandonment.

What if you freely give yourself and then are hurt? What if your husband can't be the person you want him to be? What if he can't meet your needs? The very closeness and healing you may so long for requires the ability to release those fears and dramatically give yourself during sex.

Keith had used porn as a preadolescent to self-soothe as a compensation for lack of closeness with either parent. As therapy progressed, Keith revealed that he was masturbating to porn several times a day. Mary was shocked; she had an overwhelming feeling of personal rejection. She thought that the reason Keith was using porn rather than having sex with her was that she was not measuring up to the women he was seeing in the porn.

Like Mary and Keith, you or your husband may have brought baggage into your marriage that keeps you from being able to give yourself. You may put up walls to protect from hurt. You may avoid being intimate because you fear you will lose rather than gain.

It can be a vicious cycle: Because you fear losing, you don't risk intimacy, which would give you what you so desire. Jesus teaches us in Matthew 10:39 that the only way we will gain is by being willing to lose:

He who has found his life will lose it, and he who has lost his life for My sake will find it. (NASB)

Or as *The Message* translates this verse:

> If your first concern is to look after yourself, you'll never find yourself. But if you forget about yourself and look to me, you'll find both yourself and me.

In our book *The Married Guy's Guide to Great Sex*, we say: Know yourself, open your heart, share yourself, and the comfort of closeness will follow.[2]

You may put up walls to protect from hurt.

If all people were raised in a perfect world with perfect parenting, perfect teachers, perfect friends, and perfect siblings, intimacy fulfillment would flow easily, but that is not reality. Stuff happens. And that stuff can get in the way of capacity for intimacy.

Lack of Bonding in Infancy

The next chapter will address the need to heal from various wounds or hurts. One of those hurts is not having successfully mastered one or more of the necessary stages of sexual development. If, like Keith, you did not bond or attach intimately with a loving mother or parental figure during your first year of life, you will have learned to survive without intimacy and will likely have difficulty being intimate with your husband. You may not even like to be touched.

One situation that leads to lack of bonding in infancy is the loss of a mother and no replacement for her role. It may be that she died soon after you were born or she was ill during that time, or for other reasons wasn't able to be close to you—to hold you closely, sing to you, empathize with you when you cried, and deeply connect with you in a secure, caring way.

You may have been hospitalized as a premature baby or for other medical issues. Maybe your mother wasn't able to take you to her breast for feeding, nurturing, closeness, and intimacy.

Since you won't remember that first year of life if you haven't been told about it, you may need to ask relatives or others who knew your family at that time. The fifteen-minute daily practice of our Formula for Intimacy will be extremely important for you to learn to bond.

Trauma

Have you experienced any personal violation or emotional injury from sexual, verbal, or physical abuse? Were you raised in an out-of-control home as Mary was? If so, you may not feel safe losing yourself with your husband sexually because your world was not a safe place.

If you were wounded in a dating relationship—especially if it was your first love and you opened your heart to this person and then were hurt by rejection, unfaithfulness, meanness, or controlling behaviors—you may have shut the door to being vulnerable and intimate with your husband, even if he is a safe person for you.

It could be that events in your marriage have blocked you from feeling totally free to be connected and comfortable sharing yourself with your husband because he has not been safe for you.

Pornography

This is the most common block to intimacy. Pornography is the exact opposite of intimacy; it is the erotic without connection to oneself or to another person.

Women who experienced their first arousal and release in response to an external stimulus like pornography report being unable to let go during sex with their husband unless they fantasize the pictures they saw at a vulnerable age of development. They can't lose themselves during sex in marriage because their response is connected to an unnatural, nonintimate, nonpersonal stimulus.

> Pornography is the exact opposite of intimacy.

If this is true for you, you can recondition your sexual response through the sexual retraining process we've detailed in our book *Restoring the Pleasure*,[3] or through sexual therapy.

Young men today report that pornography use has made it difficult for them to be intimate. They may continue their habit of self-stimulation in response to pornography, and struggle with erectile dysfunction when with the woman they love intimately. Their arousal is programmed to nonintimate stimuli.

"The majority of the men we see in treatment are between the ages of 35 and 55, although those numbers have skewed younger recently, mainly because of pornography," says Robert Weiss, who founded a sexual addiction treatment center.

"I'm getting 25-year-old guys who've been looking at hardcore porn on the Internet since they were 15 and now say they have trouble with relationships. The reason for this is [that] their expectation of sexuality and orgasm is based off unrealistic imagery that produces an unnatural intensity. It's like drugs. Nobody enjoys the little things, like smelling flowers, if they're doing a lot of cocaine because why bother? Smelling a flower releases a small bit of dopamine—the brain chemical that makes us feel good—whereas cocaine releases a veritable tsunami of dopamine. So who needs flowers when you've got cocaine? And who needs a relationship when you've got hardcore porn?"[4]

If this is true of your husband as it was for Keith, he will need to seek help from a sexual addiction specialist[5] to stop the porn, and then the two of you will need to engage in sexual retraining or sex therapy to learn to be intimately sexual in your marriage.

How to Counter Obstacles to Sexual Intimacy

To counter the blocks to sexual intimacy, first stop using all nonintimate stimuli. Once that behavior is under control, you can begin the sexual retraining process by using *Restoring the Pleasure*, or you can start sexual therapy with a certified sexual therapist. Either way, you will be reconditioning the brain and body to respond within the context of a normal, intimate, committed relationship.

Accepting each other's needs for space and connection and practicing our Formula for Intimacy will also help you build intimacy in your marriage.

Within an intimate, caring marriage, needs for space and needs for connection vary; differences must be communicated and negotiated so that both spouses feel heard and affirmed.

The assumption is that women need connection and men need space. In general, that's true, but all of us ultimately have need for both. Both genders are nourished by other relationship connections and need same-sex friends with whom they can share their inner worlds.

Accept Needs for Space

Susan and Richard had scheduled time for same-sex friends in a way that did not take away from their time together as a couple.

Richard had actually been interested in porn for a time in his college years. He had attended an accountability group and was accountable to a sponsor. Richard left work earlier in the day than Susan did, so he scheduled coffee with his sponsor at the end of his workday. He also used that time to spend with friends.

Since Richard had a meeting at their church every Tuesday evening, Susan used that same time to meet up with her girlfriends. This is how Richard and Susan found space from each other for other, same-sex connections.

It's fairly well accepted that men need their space—many distance themselves and go into their "man caves." Yet not all men experience that need, and some women definitely have a need for space.

We find that women who have young children feel a greater need for space than those without children in the home. When the children are pulling on mom all day and she is rarely alone, she understandably wants a break from the kids when her husband gets home.

Accept Needs for Connection

Within marriage, women seem to need close, intimate connection before they can be sexual. And certainly, their emotions need to be in sync with their bodies, which takes more connecting and feeling loved than is typically true for men.

As we mentioned in an earlier chapter, women function on two tracks, and those tracks need to be in harmony before women are ready for sex. Men function on one track—when they are physically ready, they typically are emotionally ready.

A woman wants a husband who connects—someone who's interested in knowing about her feelings, reactions, thoughts, and intuitions.

For the woman, intimacy and good sex will develop when her husband shares his love throughout their daily life. If he shows interest in her only when he wants to have sex, sex will not be good. Intimacy is thwarted if the husband is distant, cold, or preoccupied much of the day, and then right before bed—when he wants sex—he suddenly becomes all "lovey." That isn't going to work for her, so it will not work for him. She needs someone who is attuned to her desires and is communicating his love in a way that actually shows her that he cares *about her*, not just *about sex*.

Kissing and cuddling, whether or not it leads to sex, is a way to build daily connection and intimacy. It had been a vital part of Susan and Richard's dating time, and that continued into their marriage.

On the contrary, Mary and Keith had stopped kissing in an effort to save sex for marriage. They had shut down their sexual feelings in order to control their actions. Shutting off passion was likely safer for both of them due to their family of origin issues. Yet feelings don't easily turn back on when a couple marries.

> Kissing and cuddling is a way to build daily connection.

Most women enjoy the warmth of nonsexual touch (holding and cuddling) as a precursor to stimulation and becoming aroused. It's the gentle kissing and cuddling that prepares a woman's body best for arousal and response. As the man is able to let himself relax and enjoy the pleasure of the experience rather than push for the end result, the woman will come along with him and enjoy the ride.

A woman feels connected when her husband focuses on the process of enjoying the journey of sex rather than on the goal of achieving a result. Men often will be focused on "getting her aroused" or "getting her to the point of orgasm" or "getting themselves aroused or to the point of ejaculation." And this is why it is so essential that you as a woman lead your husband with your sexuality and enjoyment of the pleasure of the process. When you do this, you not only can help him keep his pace slightly behind yours, you will develop more intimacy.

What is true for you and your husband concerning your needs for connection and for space? It serves you best to clarify each of your needs, and then plan ways to meet both sets of needs.

When you accept the realities of who you are and how you each find your way to intimacy, and then bring those differences together, you will move more freely to abandoned sexual intimacy.

Practice the Formula for Intimacy

The Formula for Intimacy (see page 40) is a significant tool for building the brain's capacity to connect intimately, even for adults who missed bonding as infants or are blocked from bonding due to trauma.

Once research revealed how to encourage the brain's production of the chemical oxytocin, we were able to use that information to help spouses who had wounds from the past. As we've mentioned elsewhere, oxytocin promotes bonding, so producing more of it is a good thing! Oxytocin is also the bonding hormone of mothers and infants, produced when a mother gazes at, cuddles, and breast-feeds her baby. Infants who miss that bonding suffer as adults.

We use our formula to help adults like Richard, who didn't bond with his mother during that first year of life. Eye-to-eye communication and full body hugs are important for training people like Richard to connect intimately with a spouse.

For any couple wanting to avoid blocks to intimacy, the fifteen-minutes-per-day portion of the formula is the most important discipline for developing the capacity for intimacy. The portion of the formula that requires sharing while looking into each other's eyes may be quite uncomfortable if you have never experienced attachment or bonding as a child. Try having fun with it to move past the discomfort—play "bug-eyes" or have staring contests with each other.

The formula's spiritual connection includes God and your faith in the process of connecting. Connecting this way provides an additional level of intimacy based on your souls, rather than just your minds and bodies—and it is deep and real.

The full body, front-to-front hug portion of the fifteen minutes can be fun or tender, and it may trigger vulnerable feelings. If giving yourself fully in that way is scary, start with small steps. You might make it a short hug or not a full embrace at first. Do what you are able, and gradually increase the length of time. A more complete embrace will activate the oxytocin, the important bonding hormone.

Next comes the passionate kiss. Usually it works best if you, the woman, lead in the intensity and the duration of both the hug and the kiss. However, if your husband is the hesitant one, he should lead. Even as the hug triggers the oxytocin, the passionate kiss raises the dopamine level, which may bring back feelings of what you experienced early in your relationship. If kissing is a struggle for either of you, refer to our discussion on kissing at the end of Chapter 5.

Developing a deep intimacy between you and your husband is the key to truly becoming one. In the process of truly becoming one, you will discover the dynamic sexual relationship that ignites the spark, time after time after time. Even though sex in marriage is more of a quiet love based on oxytocin and is different from the dopamine-fueled love of new attractions,[6] it has that deep, intimate spark that continues to grow and glow over the lifetime of your marriage.

CHAPTER 8

PURSUE HEALING

To BE ABLE TO ENJOY SEX, listen to your body, lead by invitation, and be free to say no so you can enthusiastically say yes, you must first heal from any past or present hurts.

Women cannot fulfill their potential for sex in marriage until they have healed sexually. A woman needs healing if she:

- was sexually or physically abused as a child
- was a victim of trauma
- was raised in an alcoholic home
- was in an abusive relationship as an adolescent or adult
- was raped
- has physical pain during sex

If this is true of you, you will need to take the time and do the work needed to heal those wounds.

Elizabeth in our *Magic and Mystery of Sex* DVD series was the daughter of an alcoholic father and was sexually abused by her brothers while growing up. Her interest in sex shut down within weeks after she and Eric married. This pattern is typical for women who have been sexually abused in the past. Elizabeth also tenaciously resisted getting into a sexual experience with Eric. In fact, she would cause a fight to avoid sex.

If you have been hurt in the past like Elizabeth or are hurting now, it is unlikely that you can do this work of healing alone. You may need therapy provided by a professional counselor or psychologist trained in sexual therapy, as well as medical treatment, help from your husband, and ongoing participation in a group connection such as "Celebrate Recovery."[1] You will definitely need to depend upon God and support from other believers in your community as you begin your healing journey.

In this chapter, we'll explain how marital sex is affected by each of the following hurts: arrested sexual development; sexual demand and being married to an insecure, sexually needy male; past abuse experience; growing up in an alcoholic or emotionally out-of-control home; anger, shame, or guilt; inability to let go orgasmically; and physically painful sex.

Hurt: Did Not Master a Stage of Sexual Development

Based on hearing and reading many sexual histories, we have defined the stages of sexual development that need to be mastered, the learning of each stage, the parents' role, and the impact on adult sexual adjustment. This information is developed more fully in our book *Sex Facts for the Family*, available through www.passionatecommitment.com.

Mastering Sexual Development			
Stage	**Critical Learning**	**Parents' Role**	**Impact on Sexual Adjustment**
Infancy	Bonding	Attachment parenting	Capacity for intimacy
Toddlerhood	Touching, naming & control of genitals	Affirm genitals & feelings as God's special design; use correct names	Positive acceptance of genitals (user friendly)
Preschool	Question-asking, modesty	Reinforce, reflect, review, respond, repeat, respect nudity	Open communication about sex with high regard for bodies
School age	Exploring	Affirm curiosity; set boundaries; protect from abuse	Sexual awareness with boundaries and without shame
Pre-adolescence	Erotic feelings & bumbling discovery	Prepare for changes; protect from pornography; affirm God-given responses; systematic education	Self-acceptance & competence in relating to opposite sex
Adolescence	Decision-making	Share values; guide decision-making; listen!	Accept feelings; control actions

If you did not master one of these stages effectively, you may have come to adulthood with unhealthy sexual patterns. We have observed that the earlier in the developmental stages mastery is arrested, the earlier in the sexual process the response is interrupted and the more intense is the work needed to fill that gap.

Infancy: If you didn't bond and attach to a caregiver (usually your mother) during your first year of life, you may have difficulty with the intimacy of sex and may lack desire for sex with your spouse.

Toddlerhood, Preschool, and School Age: These are the curious years. If you were shamed for being curious about sex, you may connect sexual feelings and responses with shame and guilt—sex may only feel good when it is wrong.

> **Observation:**
> Sexual patterns are easily conditioned and self-perpetuating.

Preadolescence and Adolescence: If your first sexual response of orgasm or ejaculation was triggered by an external stimulus such as pornography, you still may need that stimulus to be able to respond. Women who experienced their first orgasm in response to finding pornography with pictures of nude women, for example, may need to fantasize about women's breasts or genitals to be orgasmic during sex in marriage. This leaves the woman in a lose-lose situation: She either chooses not to orgasm and is left frustrated, or chooses to emotionally leave her husband for her fantasy and is left feeling empty and guilty.

Hurt: Sexual Demand

Sexual demand is experienced in many ways.

It may be that you place demand on yourself to feel or respond in a certain way. It is common for women to enter into the "spectator role"— to watch and evaluate how they are doing during sex. They mentally stand outside the sexual experience rather than losing themselves in it.

For example, a woman may become highly aroused but not be able to let go with an orgasm because she is watching and evaluating. As she gets close to having an orgasm, rather than focusing on the good feelings, she starts to watch and wonder if she is going to have one. She may think, *Maybe this time.* The focus is on the goal rather than on enjoying the journey as described at the beginning of Chapter 5.

It may be that you feel demand from your husband. The most subtle but tenacious demand comes from a husband who is watching his wife's sexual interest in and responsiveness to him sexually. We have identified this pattern as the insecure, sexually demanding, or needy male. To find mutual sexual fulfillment in marriage, it's important to recognize and correct this pattern.

An insecure, sexually demanding, or needy male is a man who grew up without the affirmation he needed from his mother or from women in dating or in a previous marriage. He came to marriage with a "hole in his heart." He looks to fill that hole by the affirmation he will receive through his wife's sexual interest and response to him. Sex is about meeting his needs rather than about the couple freely giving themselves to each other, which over time will stifle his wife's desire and responsiveness.

> Watching and monitoring sexual responses creates demand and interferes with natural bodily enjoyment and response.

If a wife gets the message that she isn't meeting her husband's needs, she begins to feel like a failure. She will try harder to please him and do what makes him happy. But a wife of a man with this kind of hurt can never fulfill his need. That's because his need isn't about his wife, and it isn't about sex.

Since women are more easily aroused when they feel good about themselves, feeling like a failure is a recipe for an unhappy sex life. The more this wife tries and fails to please her husband, the less she enjoys—and the less she enjoys, the needier he becomes. It is a vicious, downward spiral.

This man's need for affirmation must be separated from sex. Our best resource for helping a man with this type of hurt is our book *The Married Guy's Guide to Great Sex*. Even though it's written for men, we find it most helpful for a husband and wife to read out loud together. Read it not to get through it, but as a stimulus for discussion. If you read one paragraph that opens an hour-long discussion, you have accomplished the purpose of this assignment. Some sections will elicit discussion, others won't.

That depends on you. The information in this book *can* lead to positive changes. Here's the essence of an e-mail we received from one wife:

> *First of all, let me say "thank you" for your wonderful book* The Married Guy's Guide to Great Sex. *It has instigated one of the important emotional markers in my life. My husband heard you on Focus on the Family, bought your book, and read the entire book in less than a week. When I arrived home [one day], I was met with a dozen beautiful red roses and your book. He sat me down and summarized your book for me. He explained that he was relinquishing his "right," and that he never wanted me to think of sex as a "duty" again. We are now in the process of working through your book* Restoring the Pleasure, *in hope of finding new ways to connect that are intimate and good for both of us.*

Another couple was able to correct a problem with sexual demand, which allowed the wife to find her sexual "voice." This couple had been married twenty years; the husband felt rejected by what they had both defined as her lack of interest in sex. The wife had been very interested in sex initially, but it seemed that regardless of her interest, it was never enough for her husband. So over time, she felt pressured and negatively evaluated by him, which did, indeed, decrease her interest in being with him sexually.

After working through the issues each of them brought to their marriage and taking them through the sexual therapy process of learning to give and receive touch and caressing without demand, we gave them each an assignment.

His role was to initiate fifteen minutes of connection per day following the prescription of our Formula for Intimacy on page 40. Her role was to initiate twenty minutes of sexual play every morning that did not need to lead to arousal, orgasm, or intercourse. This husband also needed to let his wife lead in intensity and activity, and to never take the lead or get ahead of her.

After a while, we received this e-mail from her: "My daily thoughts have been much more about feeling my own desires and needs, and I have not felt obligated. I have been feeling like I want sex every day, which in and of itself seems like a good thing, but I am concerned that I may be setting a precedent."

We encouraged her to listen to her inner drive and enjoy it without monitoring it mentally, and to let her husband know she was doing that. We also encouraged this wife to simply enjoy the feast with her husband, while assuring her that it would not set a precedent.

Later, she e-mailed us again: "Thanks. This seems to be a great 'problem to have.' I have been going for it and communicating with him. It has slowed down a little, but we are still enjoying ourselves without pressure or demand."

It's not always that easy to turn a sexual demand pattern around. The hurts can be deep, and both husband and wife will need a great deal of empathy and space to discover how to heal.

Hurt: Past Abuse

A person who has experienced past abuse typically shows high interest in sex before and outside of marriage; that desire shuts down within marriage.

There are two reasons we believe this happens:

1. Sex responses that occurred during the abuse became paired with negative feelings, so this woman can't have or enjoy those responses with the husband she loves.
2. In the abuse, she felt powerless and trapped. So she can easily feel that way once married because sex is expected and is no longer in her control.

The abuse has to be dealt with in talk therapy, in a group, through writing about it, or in any other way that will help a woman release the negative feelings of the abuse and no longer allow them to control her. A trauma therapy specialist is most helpful.

Once the abuse has been worked through, sexual retraining is helpful and effective. Here are the basic principles of this type of retraining:

- The physical involvement starts with what feels safe for the wife, and gradually builds so that she can connect with her husband and disconnect from the abuser and the abuse.

- She is encouraged to keep her eyes open and focused on her husband's eyes.

- While going through sexual retraining, she will likely identify what triggers her flashbacks and disassociation. Those particular behaviors that happened in the abuse can be avoided with her husband, and new positive behaviors can be established as part of their loving relationship.

- She is encouraged to develop signals to interrupt any negative sexual touch or behavior immediately.

- It is important that the couple avoid an experience in which the wife feels sex is being done to her.

If you were abused, talk about that abuse with someone you trust. If you have never shared this information with your husband, we would encourage you to do so, unless you think that doing so would not be safe or he would not be able to handle it. If you can't share with your husband, do find help. That helper will be able to guide you in how best to introduce the topic to your husband in a helpful manner.

Hurt: Adult Child of an Alcoholic

Men and women raised in an alcoholic or emotionally out-of-control home will tenaciously resist getting into a sexual experience, because they fear the feeling of being out of control.

But when they allow stimulation and become aroused, they can let go. Afterward, they shut down immediately and don't want to have those feelings again. This can be confusing to spouses, because externally, it looks like the adult child of an alcoholic has had a wonderful time.

For these adults, letting go and being out of control is uncomfortable, even frightening. Growing up, children need their parents to provide solid, safe boundaries so that children can bounce off those secure walls. When a parent is out of control—erratic and undependable—the child internalizes the need for control far too early.

A person is most out of control during an orgasm. So a person with this type of hurt has intense sexual ambivalence due to internal conflict. On one hand, the adult child of an alcoholic wants to have sex with his or her spouse. On the other hand, this person fights getting into a sexual experience and losing control sexually. However, he or she doesn't have difficulty letting go once arousal takes over. When we asked Elizabeth in our *Magic and Mystery of Sex* videos what happened once she got aroused, she exclaimed, "We have great sex!"

Adult Children of Alcoholics Sexual Resistance Graph

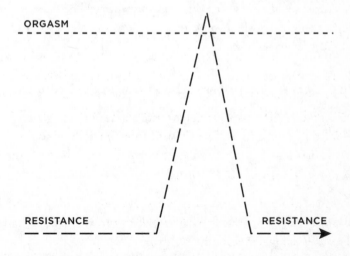

Elizabeth was able to heal when Eric, her husband, backed off completely. She was eventually able to accept his initiation of sex as she felt freed by his total acceptance.

If you were raised in an alcoholic or emotionally out-of-control home, it's best if you can make your need for control work *for* you sexually rather than *against* you. The negative feeling of being out of control will lessen over time as you take control of your sexual times. Even though it may be difficult, we encourage you to make the *decision* to be sexual and go for it.

Knowing the reason behind your discomfort helps. It will also help to remind yourself that you are no longer in a situation with an out-of-control parent. Think of yourself as the adult who is in control, and talk to the child inside you, who still behaves as if her environment is not safe.

When you make the decision to be sexual with your husband, take charge of your sexual life and ask him to back off so you can use your need for control in a positive way. Schedule your sexual times. It is best to plan to have sex once or twice a week, so you don't have time between sexual events to build up your resistance. Plan when and where sex will take place, as well as the sexual activities and what will be the best conditions for you. Even when you take charge, it is likely you will have to push beyond your resistance.

Hurt: Anger, Shame, or Guilt Have Invaded the Bedroom

As one woman explained: "He doesn't care about me until we get into bed. I'm so hurt and angry, I don't want to have anything to do with him." She may have felt like creating a barbed wire fence between them.

Anger

If you came into the relationship with anger and have directed your anger toward your husband, the conflict between you will have led to sexual avoidance. Either together or on your own, seek help from a counselor.

"APPARENTLY I HAVE DONE SOMETHING TO UPSET YOU."

Shame and Guilt

Shame and guilt are closely connected. We think of guilt as a morally wrong action and shame as feeling badly about ourselves as the result of that wrong. Sexual guilt and shame, whether authentic or inauthentic, will restrict freedom in the bedroom.

When Annie was six years old, she and her same-age male neighbor were checking out each other's genitals, a very normal expression of developmental curiosity. Parents found them during their exploratory play. Annie was spanked, shamed, and blamed for the activity. In contrast, her male friend was referred to as "such a young man."

Annie came to us after several failed marriages due to her difficulty with sex in marriage. Shame and blame were so deeply connected with sexual activity as a woman that she could never focus on sexual pleasure.

By realizing the source of her issues, and by taking small steps to healing, she learned to enjoy some pleasure and accept that enjoyment as good and of God. When her shame history clicked in with flashbacks, she learned to signal her husband and change their activity to diffuse her negative thoughts.

Inauthentic shame is shame placed on you by a message similar to what Annie experienced. The message might be that to be a sexual person or to enjoy sex is shameful, so that anything sexual—even with your husband—elicits inauthentic shame.

It could also be that you experience shame as the result of what was done to you. If you were violated and felt it was your fault, you may feel inauthentic guilt that you did something wrong—and then feel shame. It was not your fault! First Corinthians 3:16-17, as stated in *The Message*, can be helpful: "You realize, don't you, that you are the temple of God, and God himself is present in you? No one will get by with vandalizing God's temple, you can be sure of that. God's temple is sacred—and you, remember, *are* the temple."

Authentic guilt and shame may be the result of choices you made that you believe were wrong, so you carry guilt about your actions. Forgiveness and release from these emotions is available. If you are a follower of Jesus, remind yourself that He gave His life so that everyone who believes in Him can be set free from failures. Whatever your faith, seek forgiveness and release of the shame so that you can experience sexual joy and fulfillment with your husband.

Some sexual behaviors could lead to either authentic or inauthentic guilt or shame. Masturbation is one of those behaviors.

You may have engaged in self-stimulation as a very natural response to the sexual drive God created in you. The behavior was not in response to pornography or any other external, unnatural stimulus, and wasn't a withholding from your husband sexually, so it's not condemned or warned against in Scripture. Yet you feel inauthentic guilt and shame because you were taught that this was immoral self-pleasure.

On the other hand, you may feel guilt and shame for engaging in self-stimulation in response to an external stimulus and choosing that sexual release rather than intimacy with your husband.

If you live with sexual guilt or shame, determine if it is authentic or inauthentic. Paul Tournier's great book *Guilt and Grace: A Psychological Study*[2] is a helpful resource. You can take steps to be free of both guilt and shame so you can unreservedly enjoy sex with your husband.

Are you in conflict about being a sexual person? Any of the previously discussed hurts could cause an internal conflict about being sexual. Or you could have been raised in a home that discouraged or disparaged sexuality. It could be that you witnessed disturbing and inappropriate sexual behavior. These experiences may have created confusion that would make it difficult for you to see yourself as a sexual person or to enjoy sex in marriage.

It is a "Yes" and a "No" battle inside you. It's not a conflict between you and your spouse; it's a conflict within you. One side of you is saying sex is bad, dirty, scary, and to be avoided; the other side is hoping to enjoy sexual freedom with your husband. Work through that conflict with a professional who can help you release negative thoughts and accept your sexuality as something wonderful to be fully enjoyed with your husband.

Hurt: Sex is Physically Painful

Sex was designed for bodily pleasure. If you experience pain associated with your genitals and sex, the pain issue needs to be resolved before you engage in the activities that elicit the pain.

Work with a physician who specializes in dyspareunia, the technical term for painful intercourse. Before your appointment, define exactly *where* it hurts. Is it on the outside, around the opening of the vagina? At the entrance to the vagina? Along the wall of the vagina?

With a hand mirror and a cotton swab,

Sex is for pleasure; pain interrupts pleasure; painful sex cannot be allowed to continue.

position yourself sitting with legs spread, and use the mirror so you can see your genitals. Tap the cotton swab around the opening for the vagina. Identify where on the opening the tap triggered pain. Inform the physician. It might be at twelve o'clock, or any other point on the "clock."

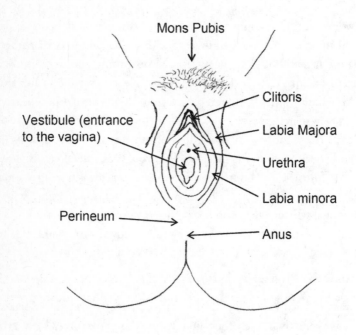

Mons Pubis

Clitoris

Vestibule (entrance to the vagina)

Labia Majora

Urethra

Labia minora

Perineum

Anus

What triggers the pain? Does tight clothing rubbing between your legs cause pain? Is entry painful? Or is it thrusting that irritates? Maybe it hurts when your husband thrusts deeply? Do you experience an ache after sex?

What type of pain is it? Is it a deep stabbing pain? Or more like a rug burn along the wall of the vagina? Does it feel like tightness and stretching?

Knowing the details of the pain will aid in getting the help you need to find relief.

Vulvar Pain

The vulva consists of the female external genitals. So vulvar pain, vulvodynia, is pain in the area around the opening of the vagina, not inside the vagina.

The vulva is comprised of many different structures, the most important of which are:

- *Mons pubis:* A rounded mass of fatty tissue at the top of the vulva that is covered with hair.

- *Labia majora, or outer lips:* Two hair-bearing external folds of skin or lips.

- *Labia minora, or inner lips:* Two flaps of hairless skin that lie within the labia majora. The flaps meet at the top, forming the hood of the clitoris, and extend downward around the vaginal opening. They meet again below the opening of the vagina.

- *Vestibule:* The area between and surrounding the labia.

- *Bartholin's glands:* A pair of glands, one on each side of the vaginal opening, that secrete lubricating mucus during sexual arousal.

- *Clitoris:* A small mass of erectile tissue at the top of the vulva that becomes engorged with blood during sexual stimulation.

Vestibulitis is an inflammation, redness, and irritation of the area around the opening of the vagina (a nonspecific irritation on the outside). *Urethritis* is an inflammation of the urethra, the tube that carries urine from the bladder to the outside of the body during urination. When you tap the cotton swab around the opening of the vagina, urethritis is likely to trigger a sharp pain at the twelve o'clock position, while vestibulitis is likely to trigger pain along the sides of the opening of the vagina, sometimes at the four and eight o'clock areas.

COTTON SWAB INDENTIFICATION OF VESTIBULITIS & URETHRITIS

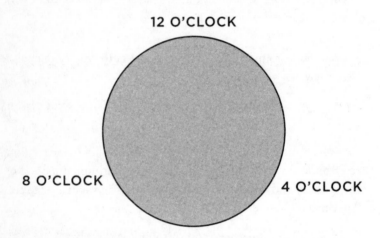

Pain of the Vaginal Barrel: Vaginitis and Vaginismus

Vaginitis is similar to vestibulitis and urethritis, except it is an internal inflammation and irritation along the vaginal wall.

Vaginismus is different from vaginitis; it is muscle tightness. The lower one-third of the vagina is either rigidly tight or spastically contracting. Treatment includes the use of graduated dilators to stretch the opening and pelvic floor physical therapy to treat the muscular issues. This very effective treatment is described in detail in our book *Restoring the Pleasure*.[3]

VAGINISMUS

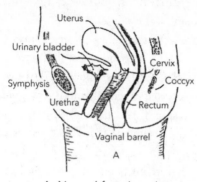
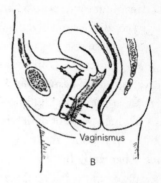

A. Normal female pelvis

B. Involuntary constriction
of outer third of vagina

Pain of the Pelvic Cavity and Structure

This pain can be due to trauma during childbirth, other injury, or a retroverted (tipped) uterus. A retroverted uterus is tipped toward the rectum rather than toward the belly; the cervix (opening of the uterus) is hit during deep thrusting. You can prevent the pain by changing positions during intercourse to avoid hitting the cervix and doing exercises to strengthen the pelvic floor, or by working with a pelvic floor physical therapist.[4]

Do not continue to engage in any sexual activity that triggers pain, because pain perpetuates more pain. Help is available. Treatment of pain in this area has improved greatly with the rise of pelvic floor physical therapists.

Hurt: Can't Let Go Orgasmically

Do you have difficulty letting go?

If you rarely or never experience orgasm, you may experience frustration, disappointment, pressure to try to make it happen and, eventually, lack of desire to get into a sexual experience because you want to avoid those feelings.

Men and women were created to experience arousal and release; both are involuntary responses that we can't choose, but we can provide the right conditions to encourage them.

An orgasm is really a pelvic sneeze. You can't make yourself sneeze, nor would you tend to stop your sneeze. It feels good to get that release and decrease the congestion in your nasal passageways. Likewise, the orgasmic release is essential to fulfilling your sexual potential, and it feels good!

To help your body learn to respond, spend some time getting to know your body. You may have done some of that already after reading Chapter 1. But in case you haven't, start with a genital self-exam. We have explicit instructions for that in our books *Restoring the Pleasure* (page 164) and *The Gift of Sex* (pages 45–46). There are also online sites to guide you.[5]

Once you've done a self-exam, experiment with what brings you pleasure and what brings arousal. You may start with self-discovery or by exploring with your husband, whichever is more comfortable for you.

> An orgasm is really a pelvic sneeze.

Consider what type of touch is best for you on your breasts, genital area, vagina, and clitoris. Many women report not getting enough of the right clitoral stimulation, so experiment and pay attention to what feels right for you. You might also explore G-spot stimulation. If you experiment on your own, share what you learned with your husband.

The next step is to incorporate what you have learned in your exploration during love play. Include various types of clitoral stimulation throughout.

When you are aroused—but before you reach the point where you are likely to shut down—get active! Get into the top position, thrust more vigorously, talk more, and practice the orgasmic triggers of pointing your toes, throwing your head back, grimacing your face, making noises, and closing your eyes tight or opening your eyes wide. Be conscious, deliberate, and active in going after what your body desires. If you feel like breathing, breathe more intensely; if you feel like thrusting, thrust more vigorously.

If you've never have an orgasm in any way, those neural pathways have not been developed. You may need practice frequently as you train your body to respond correctly. You want your body to build up enough vasocongestion to trigger the reflex of the orgasm—that's the goal of your practice.

Are You on Medication?

A number of medications reduce sexual drive as well as hinder sexual response. SSRIs (selective serotonin reuptake inhibitors) such as Prozac and Zoloft are known offenders. All of us are affected by medication in unique ways, so be sure to look up the side effects and speak to your pharmacist or your physician about your medications.

Resolving Hurts

If you and/or your husband are experiencing hurt from the past or the present, or if you have other issues that interfere with your sexual enjoyment and response, be encouraged that there is help available—you only need to pursue it. Sexual therapy or self-help sexual retraining[6] can help you *interrupt* tenacious negative patterns. It can also help both of you to *retrain yourselves* to behave and communicate in ways that develop positive sexual patterns.

Experiencing the change will be so encouraging for you and for your husband. Sexual therapy is deeply rewarding work for us, since we see how people can change negative patterns that were learned early in life. We also hear of those who have used resources such as this book to break those patterns and recondition their bodies so they have a mutually fulfilling sex life. You, too, can find the positive responses and enjoyment God intended for you. Go for healing!

CHAPTER 9

EMBRACE DIFFERENCES

WHAT KEEPS DEEP CONNECTION from happening more often in marriage?

As unique individuals and as different genders, we perceive love, life, and sex so differently, yet those very differences are key to a vibrant sexual life in marriage and to establishing healthy relationships in general. When we're able to approach our differences as assets to be negotiated, rather than rights to fight for, we discover new excitement.

Men and women *are* different, and often those differences aren't understood and embraced. Yet typical male-female differences are not true for all men or for all women.

So as you read the differences we address in this chapter, affirm the ones that apply to you and your husband, and point out those that are not true for you.

Emotional/Relational Differences

Men tend to connect side by side through an activity, so planning an activity that you both enjoy might be a way to start your connection. As you do that, flow into a face-to-face conversation since women tend to connect that way. Eventually, eye contact will be important for both of you.

In everyday life, having this connection might mean washing the dishes together, and then looking at each other over the pots and pans while you have a conversation.

Ellen felt unloved by Tim. She desperately wanted to have time to hold hands and talk about their day. She thought that if he loved her, he would automatically initiate these times to connect with her. After attending a talk Joyce gave to a group of wives about the differences between men and women, Ellen decided she needed to ask Tim for time to talk and connect. Tim was happy to engage. Ellen e-mailed us later, telling us how thrilled she was to have this information. It had made a big difference in their marriage.

Men and women process information differently.

How you each handle disappointment may also differ. Research on adolescent boys and girls indicated that when boys are upset they isolate; when girls are upset they call their friends. That was certainly true in our home.

Dr. Carol Gilligan (formerly from Harvard University, now a law professor at New York University), popularized the notion that men and women have different forms of moral reasoning. According to Gilligan, women operate primarily from an "ethic of care," taking into account the circumstances and people involved. Men, however, tend to reason from an "ethic of justice," applying universal rules to all situations.[1] Men often express that sex is their right—they operate on the basis of justice, while women need to feel cared for to open up sexually.

After UCLA neuroanatomist Laura Allen studied brains in autopsy labs and from MRI (magnetic resonance imaging) pictures, she found that men and women process information differently.

The parts of the brain that pass information from one side of the brain to the other are significantly larger in women. Female brains have more gray matter, the active brain cells that perform thinking. The rate of blood flow and the electrical activity of the female brain are quicker than they are in the male brain.

Because men have the ability to concentrate activity in one side of the brain, they tend to dominate in fields such as mathematics, which require that type of thinking. Women tend to communicate and make decisions by looking at and balancing all contributing factors, and they do more "possibility" thinking. Men tend to compartmentalize their thoughts and can become annoyed with a woman's integrative approach to thinking.[2] Accepting these differences and working with them greatly enhances a couple's communication.

Even though men are thought to be as good as women are at recognizing and detecting emotions, women are more expressive. Men use two emotional words per minute; women use three emotional words per minute.[3]

Typically, when a woman has a problem, she needs to be understood—she wants her husband to empathize with her. But instead, her husband is quick to find a solution, mistakenly believing that his wife thinks as he does and is simply looking to fix the problem.

When the husband has a problem, his wife offers understanding and help, but he wants to solve it himself. This is why men typically resist asking for directions. When a wife offers help to resolve her husband's problem, he easily feels disapproval and becomes defensive. This might be because she sends a judgmental message in her attempt to help, or that he feels inadequate when she offers help. She wants to talk about the problem, often in global terms; he thinks she is implying that he is the reason for her trouble.

When dealing with emotions, men get a lump in the throat (choked up with emotion) 29 percent of the time, while women get a lump in the throat 50 percent of the time and cry four times as often as men. A research study examining the emotional expressivity of men and women on social networking sites such as Facebook and Twitter validated these conventional findings.[4]

Men are by nature conquerors/hunters; women are nurturers by nature. Men often act as if they know it all, and then women feel invalidated. Men use humor more often than women do to influence people. Compared with men, women use facial expression and body language more often to influence others. I (Joyce) remember our son explaining to our soon-to-be son-in-law that he would know I was upset when I had "that expression" on my face. I had never known my emotion was that obvious.

Which of these differences apply to you and your husband? You might have fun going through these emotional/relationship differences together, as long as there isn't blame, defensiveness, and criticism in the process. The point is this—knowing these differences can lead to understanding.

Hormonal Differences

Compared with a woman's body, a man's body has one-fifth as much estrogen, one-tenth as much progesterone, and fifteen times more testosterone. PMS affects one of every three women in their thirties and forties. Symptoms include anxiety, irritability, mood swings, cravings, fatigue, depression, bloating, and weight gain.

Sexual Differences

These differences are more subjective and less researched. Men are typically more visual; women are relational. A man becomes aroused when he sees his wife; a woman is aroused when her husband affirms her and she feels good about herself.

The longer the time between sexual experiences, the wider the gap between men and women. The man is more eager and responds more quickly; the woman is less interested and takes longer to become aroused and respond. A group of men expressed an "aha" moment when Cliff taught them that they would need to take more time with their wives if it had been a while since they'd had sex. In these situations, men also need to accept that they may have more difficulty delaying ejaculation.

Men and women also differ in their physiological responses, although there are many similarities, and the phases of the sexual response cycle are the same in men and women.

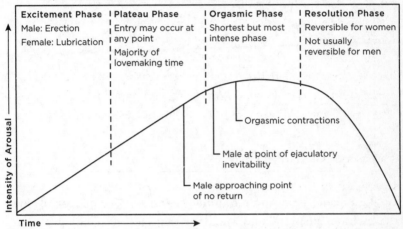

SEXUAL RESPONSE PATTERN
Adapted from Masters and Johnson, *Human Sexual Response* (Boston: Little, Brown, and Company, 1966).

If a man responds with his natural tendency, his sexual response graph looks like this:

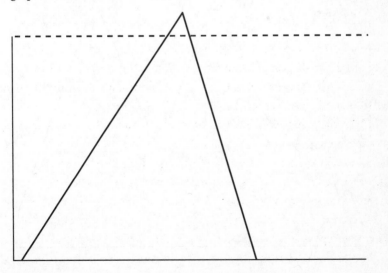

A woman's natural way to go through the phases of the sexual response cycle is in waves. Her response looks like this:

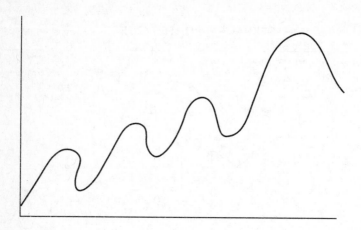

Unlike a man, a woman can continue her orgasm without completing the resolution phase. While he needs to wait, she can be restimulated to another orgasm or continue to respond with an extended orgasm. That's why women can have multiple orgasms that look like this:

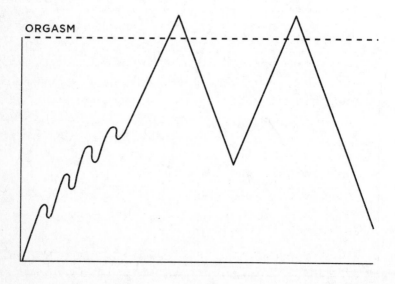

Or extended orgasms that look like this:

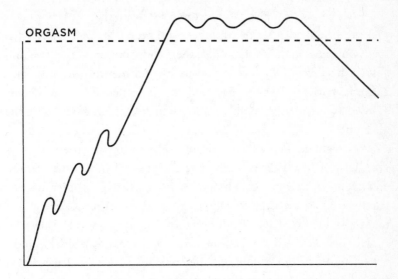

ORGASM

Men have more performance pressure for getting and keeping erections and for learning to delay ejaculation because men tend to be active rather than passive. Women have more performance pressure for having an orgasm because women tend to be passive rather than active.

Men are more predictable than women are. In his book *Men Are from Mars, Women Are from Venus*, John Gray says that men are like the sun—they rise every morning and set every evening; women are like the moon—they change every day of the month. A man tries to figure out what his wife wants sexually, and just when he thinks he has it, she changes. So he is consistently playing "Find the Button." Yet we find that:

> The combination of a woman's ever-changing, complex
> femininity and a husband's predictableness can be used to keep
> sex alive in marriage rather than cause conflict and tension.

When a woman accepts that her husband is going to be more predictable and gives herself permission to lead with her ever-changing complexity during sex, the couple's sexual experiences will be more enjoyable for both.

As we counsel couples, women often complain that sex is boring or their husbands do the same thing every time. When we explore what these women would like and nudge them to try out their ideas, we find that husbands typically love the creativity, and the women find a new enthusiasm for sex. Women may need new and different ways to become aroused, while men seem able to be stimulated in the same way time after time.

You might not know what you would like, so you may need to experiment. Try new ways to awaken your awareness of your sexual desires. You might try listening to your body as you learned in Chapter 2, wearing something sexy, using new makeup, or remembering positive sexual times with your husband. Find something that makes you feel alive!

Not only are we different as men and women, but we differ as individuals, also. The most common differences are desired frequency of sex, how initiation happens, and preferred sexual activities.

Frequency

The one who wants sex more often tends to believe the other never wants it. The one who wants sex less often tends to believe that sex is all the other wants. So without discussion, you and your husband should each write down how often you want sex and how often you think the other wants sex. Using the effective communication skills presented in Chapter 6, compare your perspectives, focusing on understanding each other's answers rather than on being understood.

Initiation

When we ask spouses to indicate how often they each initiate sex, the combined percentage usually exceeds 100 percent; both believe they initiate more than is perceived by the other. This may also be true for the two of you. Each should write out the percentage you believe you initiate. Then compare and talk about *how* you initiate sex.

We suspect that since women initiate more subtly and men more overtly, each attributes sexual events to his or her initiation. The husband likely takes credit for his overt initiation

Talk about how you initiate sex.

that happened in response to his wife's subtle message. Share and clarify how and when initiation works best for each of you. If you wish to change your initiation pattern, complete the homework assignment in Appendix 3.

Sexual Activity Choices

Most spouses have some conflict about specific sexual activities. We are often asked whether certain sexual activities, from a spiritual perspective, are okay for a married couple to enjoy. Since the Bible doesn't offer any specific direction regarding sexual activity within marriage, we refer to the model given in the Song of Solomon. We've created guidelines that we believe are scripturally based.

GUIDING PRINCIPLES FOR SEXUAL ACTIVITIES IN MARRIAGE

1. *Is it loving?* Does it fit the qualities listed in 1 Corinthians 13?
2. *Is it mutual?* Is it as good for one as it is for the other?
3. *Does it build intimacy?* Does it bring you closer together? For example, secular research shows that couples who watch pornography together have intense erotic experiences, but over time lose their ability to respond to each other. So that activity interferes with, rather than builds, intimacy.
4. *Does it in any way distance you from God or violate any biblical principle?* For example, self-stimulation in marriage violates a biblical principle if one spouse chooses that means to sexual fulfillment when the other spouse would like to be together sexually. Scripture teaches that spouses are to give themselves freely to each other.

So we conclude that it is best to *go with the most sexually conservative spouse, allowing that person to take small steps toward comfort with a sexual activity if it fits the above criteria.* The spouse who is uncomfortable with the activity the other desires defines his or her inhibition on the left of the steps on the chart on page 11 and the freedom desired on the right side. The desired freedom does not need to be the activity the other spouse desires. As a couple, you may need to compromise so both can enjoy the activity.

As you work out and embrace your differences, keep in mind the following four observations and truths about the differences between men and women. When these differences are honored, we've found they promote mutual sexual fulfillment in marriage:

- Nothing arouses a man more than an aroused woman.

- Women become aroused when they feel good about themselves.

- So the man's role is to affirm his wife for who she is as a person and for who she is sexually. Scripture validates this finding: "Husbands, go all out in your love for your wives, exactly as Christ did for the church—a love marked by giving, not getting. Christ's love makes the church whole. His words evoke her beauty. Everything he does and says is designed to bring the best out of her, dressing her in dazzling white silk, radiant with holiness. And that is how husbands ought to love their wives. They're really doing themselves a favor—since they're already 'one' in marriage" (Ephesians 5:25-28).

- The woman pleases her husband most when she is in touch with her sexuality and shares her sexual enjoyment with him, which is the premise of this book.

But as we have already mentioned, to be in touch with her sexuality, a woman needs to be able to receive pleasure, to believe she is worthy of her husband's touch, and has the right, potential, and ability to be intensely sexual.

She has to be able to enjoy her sexuality, her husband's sexuality, and her husband's enjoyment of her sexuality.

Sex has to be as good for her as it is for him if it is going to be good for both of them for a lifetime. Remember, 1 Corinthians 7:3 tells us, "The marriage bed must be a place of mutuality—the husband seeking to satisfy his wife, the wife seeking to satisfy her husband."

Since men and women differ in their natural response and the man isn't truly satisfied unless the woman is, he must adapt his pace to his wife's and learn to ride the waves with her. As the husband moves in the direction of his wife's natural tendencies, her heart opens to him.

She then feels more attracted to him and more interested in sex. Her sexual interest allows her to lead with her sexuality, not with demand, but by listening to her body and going after what her body desires. Then she guides him and invites him to enjoy her body, which meets her needs and makes him feel good about himself.

TO SUMMARIZE, HERE'S THE SYSTEM THAT WORKS:

The husband loves, adores, and connects with his wife;
his adoration frees her to open up sexually;
his affirmation ignites her passion;
she invites him sexually;
he feels validated.
Both end up happy—it's a win-win!

The Song of Solomon is the best example of the husband adoring and the wife inviting. He tells her everything he loves about her body, and she invites him to enjoy her body: first with kisses, then with her breasts, then her genitals (expressed as "come into my garden"), and finally inviting him to the orchard where she will give him her love, which is interpreted as the consummation of their sexual relationship.

What you need for affirmation may be different from Solomon's wife, but the two of you might read the Song out loud together and fill in your wishes for affirmation. Some women most enjoy compliments of their looks, others prefer affirmation of themselves as persons, and still others love attention to their accomplishments. What is true for you? What type of invitation would you likely use? How would your husband respond to your natural ways?

When He's Hot and You're Not

You may wish you had one of these nighties.

"HELEN TRIES OUT HER NEW "NOT-TONIGHT,-HONEY" NIGHTGOWN.

If the husband is the pursuer, he becomes angry and frustrated with his wife's lack of interest, and his wife feels guilty and inadequate. If you are not interested in sex, consider whether these questions fit you.

1. ARE YOU USING UP ALL OF YOUR ENERGY ELSEWHERE?

Our sexual energy and our drive to get things done come from the same source. For one young mother, sex is low on her list of priorities: "I have three preschool children and a husband who works long hours. I would much rather sleep than have sex." If you find yourself in this situation, we suggest finding a way to have time for yourself. Could you take a short, daily nap while the children are napping? Could you pay a student to babysit for an hour after school or trade babysitting with another mom so you can have a break? Finding time for yourself is not only a gift to yourself, but also to your children and to your husband.

2. ARE YOU HAVING SEX BY DEMAND OR DUTY?

"When we were first married, I was eager," shared one woman. "But it seems like I never could meet his needs, so now I feel so pressured that I no longer even want sex." If this describes you, you should know that sexual demands stifle desire, and sexual force-feeding leads to sexual anorexia.

It is natural to want to desire sex. But when desire isn't there, it's fine to have sex by decision. Yet *deciding* to have sex is different from having sex because of *demand* or *duty*.

- *Duty* is an attitude of obligation to have sex for him.
- *Decision* is a choice you actively make for yourself, not because of desire, but because you know sex is good for you and it's time.

But you might be thinking, *What if he wants it and I don't?* It's fine to make love with your husband when he wants to and you don't, as long as you aren't feeling negative about the possibility. In those times when you feel neutral about lovemaking, you may prefer not to go for arousal or release, and instead simply enjoy the closeness and pleasurable sensations. Choose what's best in that moment.

3. ARE YOU WAITING TO BE "ZAPPED"? ARE YOU LOOKING FOR INFATUATION OR ATTRACTION RATHER THAN ATTACHMENT?

The brain chemicals that trigger attraction are very different from those that fuel long-term attraction. Even as you can decide to have sex rather than have sex by demand or wait for desire, you do not have to be aroused to initiate sex. Many women don't feel desire until they are into a sexual experience.

This reality contradicts the messages we hear in our world. In the movies or in pornography, eyes of total strangers meet across a crowded room, and within minutes the two people are so hot with passion that they go to the nearest isolated location to make love. This is not realistic for intimate sex in marriage.

Desire for your husband may feel more like wanting a time of closeness and cuddling. That closeness may lead to wanting more, and then arousal triggers more intense desire for active sexual involvement.

4. ARE YOUR HORMONES OUT OF BALANCE?

All the effort in the world won't work if your hormones are out of balance.

Hormonal changes may affect desire and responsiveness if you are on a *hormonal birth control pill* that is high in progestin and low in estrogenic and androgenic activity. Estrogen is the "happy" hormone that also keeps the vagina lubricated and responsive. Progesterone is the "relaxation" hormone, but synthetic progestin can trigger vaginal dryness and irritation as well as stifle desire. Testosterone or androgen is the "drive" hormone that increases sexual interest and responsiveness.

Hormonal changes during *the menstrual cycle* can affect your level of interest, so keep a record of your cycle and note when your interest is higher; plan for sex during those times. (Read more about the menstrual cycle in Chapter 6.)

Hormonal changes during *pregnancy and breast-feeding* can affect your level of interest and responsiveness. Since manipulating hormones during pregnancy and breast-feeding could affect the baby, you will need to address this by simply deciding to have sex, and making it the best it can be for you given your hormone situation at that time.

Hormonal changes of *menopause* are brought about as a woman's body decreases its production of estrogen and progesterone. Since these changes increase the likelihood of pain due to decrease in vaginal lubrication and thinning of the vaginal wall, it will be important to use natural remedies or acceptable hormonal replacement. Your physician will be the best authority on what is right for you.

But there are other resources to enhance your experience and support your body through the changes of menopause. Treatment from a pelvic floor physical therapist can be beneficial. To find a pelvic floor physical therapist in your area, visit www.pelvicpain.org, go to the "Patients" tab, and click on "Find a Provider." For a supportive eating plan that can also help, see Appendix 1.

Fortunately, women's ovaries can continue to produce testosterone long after menopause, so postmenopausal women who still have their ovaries do not always experience decrease in sexual desire.

To manage hormonal changes effectively no matter your life stage, ask your doctor to order a complete hormonal panel. See Appendix 4 for a sample letter you might adapt to submit a request to your physician.

When You're Hot and He's Not

What if he has the headache?

If your husband is the avoider and you are eager, you may be angry and frustrated, or even feel unattractive. He may feel guilty and inadequate.

"My husband is exhausted from work and doesn't seem interested in sex, even when I initiate," one woman says. "I don't think he's attracted to me anymore."

We've observed that:

When women lack desire, the couple may still be having sex regularly;

when men lack desire, the couple usually is not having sex or not having it
very often.

Contrary to common belief, men are not always ready for sex. If this is true of your husband, talk with him about how he feels about sex and about your desire for sex. Would it help him if you initiated without demand whenever you would like sex? How could you do that without placing demand on him? For many men, physical initiation is more effective than verbal initiation. Complaining is a sure turn-off.

Make Your Differences Work

As you discover your differences as a man and a woman—and as individuals—decide to make them work for your relationship instead of against it. When you are able to listen accurately to each other without judgment, resolving conflicts and embracing your diversity will be easier and more effective.

> Complaining is a sure turn-off.

Negotiation *is* possible when you respect each other and work together to come to a mutual agreement. Resolving a conflict may mean you will need to agree to disagree, but not be in conflict about it.

As you learn to negotiate, be sure to avoid the known barriers to embracing differences. Dr. John Gottman's research points to four communication styles that couples should avoid. He calls them the "Four Horsemen of the Apocalypse" because their use can predict the end of a relationship. They are:[5]

1. Criticism
2. Defensiveness
3. Contempt
4. Stonewalling

In his blog, Gottman clearly defines and then shares the antidotes for fighting off the Four Horsemen as follows:[6]

Criticism: A complaint focuses on a specific behavior, while a criticism attacks the character of the person. The antidote for criticism is to complain without blame. Talk about your feelings using "I" statements and then express a positive need. What do you feel? What do you need?

- Criticism: "You always talk about yourself. You are so selfish."
- Antidote: "I'm feeling left out by our talk tonight. Can we please talk about my day?"

Defensiveness: Defensiveness is defined as self-protection in the form of righteous indignation or innocent victimhood in attempt to ward off a perceived attack. Many people become defensive when they are being criticized, but the problem is that being defensive never helps to solve the problem at hand. Defensiveness is really a way of blaming your partner. You're saying, in effect, the problem isn't me, it's you. As a result, the problem is not resolved and the conflict escalates further. The antidote is to accept responsibility, even if only for part of the conflict.

- Defensiveness: "It's not my fault that we're always late, it's your fault."
- Antidote: "Well, part of this is my problem. I need to think more about time."

Contempt: Statements that come from a relative position of superiority. Some examples of displays of contempt include when a person uses sarcasm, cynicism, name-calling, eyerolling, sneering, mockery, and hostile humor. Contempt is the greatest predictor of divorce and must be eliminated. The antidote is building a culture of appreciation and respect.

- Contempt: "You're an idiot."

- Antidote: "I'm proud of the way you handled that teacher conference."

Stonewalling: Stonewalling occurs when the listener withdraws from the interaction. The antidote is to practice physiological self-soothing. The first step of physiological self-soothing is to stop the conflict discussion. If you keep going, you'll find yourself exploding at your partner or imploding (stonewalling), neither of which will get you anywhere. The only reasonable strategy, therefore, is to let your partner know that you're feeling flooded and need to take a break. That break should last at least twenty minutes, since it will be that long before your body physiologically calms down. It's crucial that during this time you avoid thoughts of righteous indignation ("I don't have to take this anymore") and innocent victimhood ("Why is he always picking on me?"). Spend your time doing something soothing and distracting, like listening to music or exercising.

Since God created each of us as unique beings, you can expect to encounter differences in your marriage. While it's typical to want your husband to see situations in the same way you see them and to act in ways that always meet your needs, expecting that to happen only causes disappointment. Take a step toward embracing your differences by letting go of your expectations for your husband.

By recognizing and negotiating your differences, you're more likely to gain a deep sense of peace and connection with your husband and experience the excitement those differences can bring.

CHAPTER 10

PROTECT

As YOU AFFIRM your sexuality, you may be wondering if it's a safe thing to do. Will giving yourself permission to be intensely sexual tempt you to be unfaithful?

Here's the exciting answer to that concern: Accepting your sexuality and enjoying sex with your husband will actually *protect* your marriage. When you are both enjoying close, intimate times together, there's less chance that either of you will look elsewhere for that connection. And remember, sexual passion within marriage is God's design.

Sex works best when you allow yourself to have sexual desires and keep them within your marriage. But even a happy sex life with your husband does not exempt you from natural temptations. It's important to be aware of this fact and know how to protect your marriage if temptations arise. Knowing the characteristics of affairs and how certain situations can trigger them will help you protect your relationship with your husband.

Know Your Vulnerability

Protecting your marriage and keeping it safe may seem unnecessary to you. You may be strongly committed to each other and to God. Infidelity and divorce *are not* options in your marriage. That's great! But you cannot take your love and commitment for granted. You cannot assume that your love for each other is enough.

We encourage you to accept your vulnerability. Some women are shaken and question their marital love when they feel attracted to another man. They've been convinced that true love will prevent them from ever being tempted or finding other men attractive. So if a woman with this belief finds herself strongly attracted to someone else, she reasons that she must no longer love her husband.

Temptations and attractions are natural, so it's important to know how to handle them when they occur. It can be helpful to practice picturing your spouse when you find yourself responding to another man. Mentally slip his picture in place of the other person you see.

You cannot take your love for granted.

When feelings of response or attraction to another person occur, direct them toward home. Use that newness and spark with your spouse, sexually or otherwise. Act out with your spouse the feelings you experienced. Let's say you are at a business meeting or church committee meeting and the man across from you has similar characteristics to your husband. You're watching him talk and find that feeling of attraction mounting. Text your husband: "Can we play tonight? I've been thinking of you."

Remind yourself of God's promise in 1 Corinthians 10:12-13: "Don't be so naive and self-confident. You're not exempt. You could fall flat on your face as easily as anyone else. Forget about self-confidence; it's useless. Cultivate God-confidence. No test or temptation that comes your way is beyond the course of what others have had to face. All you need to remember is that God will never let you down; he'll never let you be pushed past your limit; he'll always be there to help you come through it."

Different Kinds of Affairs

Most people define an affair as having sexual intercourse or other sexual engagement with a person other than your spouse. An affair may be mostly about sex with high passion, excitement, and intensity, and without any attachment to the other person.

Yet an affair can also be defined as unfaithfulness of the heart, mind, or soul without any physical contact with another person. You might discover you have much in common with someone else and find a connection that is missing in your marriage.

An affair also can be a total-package attachment that binds you to another person at the expense of your relationship with your husband and gets in the way of your relationship with God. It may be a deep and meaningful attachment that includes spiritual, sexual, emotional, and intellectual connections. This type of affair is the most difficult to end.

Characteristics of an Affair

Affairs have several distinguishing traits. The spouse involved in an affair is usually preoccupied. His or her thoughts drift to the other person and away from the spouse. Secretiveness is usually in play, and secrets bind the two "affairees." Most affairs have an addictive component; an affair is difficult to stop. The dopamine surge of excitement from taking the risk and feeling guilt is powerful. It feels so much like love. And that "love" is blind to the flaws of the new partner. Someone having an affair uses a lot of brain energy and time as he or she plans ways to be with the other person and anticipates those times together. People are willing to give up and risk so much for momentary pleasure, which seems absolutely vital to life at that time.

What Leads to an Affair?

To prevent an affair, it's important to know what may cause it. Unresolved anger toward a spouse may justify an affair as "payback" for the offenses that triggered that anger. Unaddressed dissatisfaction in the marriage may make one vulnerable to attraction to someone else. Sometimes the spouses in the marriage have gradually drifted apart without even noticing until one spouse ends up becoming excited by someone else. And then there is the newness factor that contributes to the "grass looking greener" with a different person. Sometimes an attraction happens without any contributing factors.

Newness Excites and Hides Flaws

When you live with someone day after day, the very characteristics that once intrigued you may now be an irritation:

- Your bubbly and talkative personality may have counteracted his shyness; now your chattering irritates him.

- His methodical thinking may have seemed like a blessing since you tend to have a scattered mind-set, but now you feel controlled by his orderly ways.

- His respect of your sexual boundaries before marriage may have been a relief to you, but now his lack of sexual interest is frustrating.

- Your accepting, laid-back attitude toward life may have been a refreshing break for your husband from his compulsive personality, but now he can't stand the fact that you don't keep the house tidy.

Chemistry Attracts

Chemistry or *electricity* are terms used to describe this type of attraction. These impulsive "zap" feelings of attraction are thought to be brought on by natural chemical aphrodisiacs of the brain. Those powerful feelings have nothing to do with love, but the force of this type of infatuation can certainly be deceiving. Sara found that to be true.

"Even though I really loved my husband, I had this strong, physical attraction to a man I worked with," says Sara. "Back then I didn't know the difference between infatuation and true love, and I was confused. But once I read a book describing love as a choice, not a feeling, I decided to find a different job. My husband and I actually moved to a different town so I could get away from that temptation. That 'electric' physical attraction was powerful and deceiving, but after I decided to stay true to my wedding vows the feelings of attraction for my husband returned. We've had a great marriage and sex life over the last thirty years, and we love each other unconditionally. I wouldn't give up our deep and caring relationship for anything."

You may never be "zapped." Or it may happen once or twice in your lifetime. If it does happen, you realize that you are suddenly and dramatically "turned on" to someone, even without physical contact or stimulation. This is the most exciting and dangerous attraction, because it's so powerful and unintentional. It can be scary. You may not believe it is happening to you. It may feel like real love.

Situations May Lead to Temptation

Feelings toward a person of the opposite sex may develop when you are in a situation where you have frequent or ongoing contact with a person of the opposite sex. Attraction and attachment unexpectedly grow. It can happen so naturally. *No one is exempt!* Not you. Not your best friend. Not your spouse.

This type of situation won't happen to everyone or with every person of the opposite sex, but you can't be sure. You can work closely with some people for years and nothing happens, even though you really like and respect each other. With others, an attraction and attachment can seem so natural and almost irresistible. It happens for some people more than for others. Some look for it. Others work hard to avoid it.

> An attraction can seem so natural.

The Consequences of an Affair

If you have an affair, you deplete the marital trust "bank." Your spouse will have little trust in you. In addition, your productive energy for life can be used up by the energy it takes to have the affair. Yet some people are energized by an affair—the adrenalin boost moves a depressed person to a happy state, and he or she is actually more productive.

Although an affair is threatening to a marriage, it need not destroy it. Divorce is a common consequence, however. Marriage cannot compete with the "newness," energy, and "eros" of an affair.

The love in a marriage is so different from that of an affair. It's a quiet, deep love consisting of commitment, caring, devotion, giving, liking, sharing, and a solid, intimate passion—not an adrenaline and dopamine-fueled passion. It's not as powerful in the moment, but it's sustaining in strength.

Prevent Attacks

There are several ways to protect your marriage from attack.

- Keep your mind pure by what you put into it. Fill your mind with images of loving, fun, fantastic times with your spouse. Free your mind of input that encourages emotional, mental, or physical adultery. Run from pornography on your devices, in magazines, movies, videos, or chat rooms. Be careful about social media connections.

- Surround yourself with couples and friends who value marriage and build up their spouses. Make a speedy exit when tempted. Tell someone about the temptation (other than the person you're attracted to); build accountability into your life.

- Make a plan to counter the temptation. Rehearse the plan, including how you are going to remove yourself from the situation. Stop rehearsing the temptation in your mind.

- Pour yourself into your marriage. Act out your fantasies with your husband. Create erotic adventures with him. Shut off the distractions and plan "gourmet" sexual delights together.

Genesis describes the sexual union between a husband and wife—"becoming one flesh"—as part of God's perfect creation. This union symbolizes the connection between God and His people in the Old Testament, and between Christ and the church in the New Testament. When that sacred, sexual union in a marriage is dishonored, the sacred oneness so essential to marital union is violated.

> God gave us the capacity for fantasy and the responsibility for the content of the fantasies.

Proverbs 4:23 warns us to guard our affections, for they influence everything else in our lives. Practicing faithfulness in your mind and your actions will bring lasting joy to you as a person and in your relationship with your spouse. Becoming one with your husband and protecting your union is worth the effort!

CHAPTER 11

ACCEPT REALITY

As YOU AND YOUR HUSBAND travel through life together, it's important to be realistic about your sex life. At various stages of your lives, you'll need to make adjustments to find the best conditions for your sexual relationship.

While it's natural to strive for some ideal, setting yourselves up for unrealistic expectations will only add to your frustrations and lessen your satisfaction.

Take some time to review what we've discussed throughout this book—what sex in marriage actually is meant to be. By facing reality with your husband, you can make any needed adjustments and work together to create a mutually satisfying sex life.

Align Your Expectations

There are four realities of sex in marriage. You will need to align your expectations to these realities and with each other.

Sex Is an Expression of Love

The characteristics of love as listed in 1 Corinthians 13 are patience and kindness; not being jealous, arrogant, or self-seeking; not being easily provoked; and not calculating the wrongs but rejoicing in the positives. This is quite different from the dopamine-fueled, excited type of love.

Scripture instructs the wife to honor her husband sexually and the husband to love his wife sexually like Christ loved us and gave Himself for us without any demands (see Ephesians 5:22-25). Both spouses are to freely give themselves to each other as stated in Ephesians 5:21 ("be subject to one another," NASB), and 1 Corinthians 7:3-5 from *The Message* reminds us that husband and wife are to seek to satisfy each other and serve each other, "whether in bed or out."

The Song of Solomon is the scriptural description of a sexual relationship between a husband and wife. He expresses his love through *adoration* and affirmation; she expresses her love by inviting him to enjoy her sexually.

Sex Is for Reproduction

There is also a functional purpose to sex. In Genesis 9:7, we read that we are to be fruitful and multiply. As a woman moves from arousal toward orgasm, the lower one-third of her vagina thickens with engorgement to form the orgasmic platform that contracts during her orgasmic response; these responses are for pleasure.

The upper part of her vagina expands to form the seminal pool where her husband's seminal fluid containing sperm will be deposited when he ejaculates. Then when she has an orgasm, the uterus will lower into the seminal pool and the cervix will open to receive the sperm; this enhances the possibility of impregnation for procreation.

Sex Is for Intimacy

Sex in marriage is designed for the deep and intimate connection of "becoming one." Genesis 2:24 reads: "For this reason a man shall leave his father and his mother, and be joined to his wife; and they shall become one flesh" (NASB); Paul quotes this Genesis passage in Ephesians 5:31 in his teaching about sex in marriage. "Becoming one" is that process of husbands and wives loosing themselves and bonding deeply with each other. Research on sex and the brain has found that the brain chemicals of attraction (dopamine, adrenaline, and others) are totally different from those of attachment (primarily oxytocin). "Becoming one" is about attachment and intimacy.

Sex Is for Pleasure

The Song of Solomon is a beautiful description of a husband and wife openly and freely enjoying their bodies sexually. Read it in the paraphrase *The Message* for a vivid affirmation of sexual pleasure. Eugene H. Peterson's introduction says: "The Song . . . makes a connection between conjugal love and sex—a very important and very biblical connection to make. . . . The Song proclaims an integrated wholeness. . . . We see here what we are created for, what God intends for us in the ecstasy and fulfillment that is celebrated in the lyricism of the Song."

What is reality for you and your husband?

What is reality for you and your husband? Plan a time for the two of you to define your reality. You might start by brainstorming. Jot down every thought, whether it's kids, jobs, schedules, space, health, relationship, or something else.

For example, if you have an infant and a toddler, finding times for your sexual play will be more difficult than if you are a couple without children in the home. If you are going through medical treatment for cancer or another debilitating disease, your sexual times will be different from when you and your husband were both healthy.

Some of these situations require short-term adjustments; others may be chronic and will need long-term adaptations. Whatever your situation, you can plan sexual times to be the best they can be for the two of you and fulfill mutual desires for deep intimacy, care, and abiding love.

Questions you might include in your discussion are:

- Is one or both of you looking for "fireworks" or the dopamine-fueled spark in your relationship? This expectation might be realistic if you are newly married, but if you've been married awhile, it probably isn't.

- Are you having sex as often as you both would like? If you did the communication exercise in Chapter 6, you probably already discussed that reality. If one or both of you are not satisfied with your frequency, consider scheduling times to play. Plan one weekly time that is designed to enjoy each other without the expectation that it will lead to intercourse, arousal, or orgasm. Allow for that possibility if it becomes a mutual desire during your scheduled enjoyment of each other.

- Are both or one of you dealing with the sexual changes resulting from aging or illness? If so, how are you or might you adapt your expectations in light of those issues?

It may help you to be aware of sexual changes common to men and women as they enter the senior years.

A man's testosterone reaches its peak in his midtwenties and decreases at one percent per year on the average, so at age fifty it will be 25 percent lower than it was at age twenty-five. Some men don't notice a difference at that age, but many do start sensing the changes, which are:

- He may no longer come to the sexual experience already aroused, but may need penile stimulation to get and keep an erection. Some men interpret that change as a loss in desire or experience it as sexual dysfunction. It is neither. Women often appreciate this change because he now responds more the way she does.

- His erections may not be as firm as they once were, but if he has good blood flow to the penis, he may be able to have firm enough erections to have entry. If that is no longer possible, it is important that he have a thorough medical evaluation by a urologist who is familiar with testing for erectile dysfunction. Since erectile response is due to the supply of blood to the penis, inability to have an erection could be a warning of a heart condition. His cardiac functioning will need evaluation.

- It may take longer for him to ejaculate, and he may not need to ejaculate with each sexual experience. Accepting that reality will put less pressure on both of you. Some men keep vigorously thrusting, which then causes vaginal irritation for the aging wife.

- The ejaculation will not be as intense. When we went to the Masters and Johnson Institute for training, Masters said: "A twenty-year-old spurts; a fifty-year-old dribbles."

- It will take longer to get another erection after an ejaculation. In fact, it will likely take hours—maybe even days.

- With a physician's determination and prescription, the changes of aging may be treated with Androgel, a testosterone supplement, and with an oral erectile conditioner like Viagra, Cialis, or Levitra.

If a woman still has her ovaries, her testerone levels may not change much until after age sixty-five. Her changes will be due to decrease in estrogen and progesterone. Hormone replacement therapy (HRT) is practiced cautiously now, due to findings that associate HRT with increased risk of breast cancer and other medical issues.

Other recommendations for women's physical changes are outlined in Appendix 1 or have been referred to previously. The primary difficulties for aging women are decrease in lubrication and the thinning of the vaginal wall, which may lead to vaginal irritation and pain.

Adjust to Realities

Following are adjustments to the realities of sex and of marriage that younger, newly married couples typically need to address.

SEX IS MESSY! ENJOY THE MESS!

Women lubricate, some women ejaculate; they have what is called a flooding response. You need to protect the bed for this. The liquid comes out of the urethra, but it is not urine. It can be as much as one-third cup, so that will be messy.

Men ejaculate, and even though it's only a teaspoon it can feel like a mess. If you are a woman who never likes to get messy, you may need to do some play therapy with your husband. Play with clay, goo, or wet sand. Learn to let the juice from the orange run down your arm as you eat it. Laugh, giggle, and enjoy at your pace.

Your circumstances will change.

Be sure your husband knows not to force you into messes, which may trigger more dislike rather than warm you to the experience of sexual body secretions. Find creative ways to open your eyes, your heart, and your mind to the possibility that messes are a positive part of the sexual experience.

YOU MARRIED A REAL PERSON!

Your husband in not the fantasy person you may have created in your mind. And you are not the fantasy person he may have created in his mind. Harville Hendrix's book *Getting the Love You Want*[1] is a great resource if you find yourself questioning your choice and having difficulty with reality.

Flow with the Changes

Throughout a lifetime, your circumstances will change. It may be that when you first married, one of you attended school while the other was working. Later, there may have been fertility struggles when sex became about work to make a baby. If you are in that situation now, separate baby-making sex from pleasure-for-you sex. Take time for both.

Pregnancy presents a new set of circumstances. Some women become more aroused when they're pregnant and desire more sex than ever; for others, the hormonal changes we mentioned in an earlier chapter can shut down sexual interest and response. Many studies indicate that frequency of sex is cut in half after the first child arrives. And when another child comes along, finding time for yourselves becomes even more challenging.

There may be a bit of a reprieve when the children are all in school, but then they become adolescents, which presents different challenges. Finding your sexual rhythm may be even more difficult. Your kids may be going to bed later than you would like to go to bed.

When you become empty nesters, hopefully you will have kept in touch with each other sexually, rolled with the changing life circumstances, and maintained your sexual relationship. Then you will have the joy of rediscovering sex with freedom in your home. It is a joy!

CHAPTER 12

KEEP LEARNING

Do you have questions about your sexual relationship that we haven't yet addressed?

Hopefully the following "what-if" questions and answers will help. If you have more questions that aren't answered here or in other chapters, feel free to contact us at www.passionatecommitment.com.

No matter what, decide to keep learning as you discover your God-given sexuality and share yourself fully with your husband.

What if "going for it" is giving in to him? You know your husband would like sex, but you find yourself avoiding and resisting sex even though you really would enjoy it. What is that about?

You may be angry with him because of unresolved problems in your relationship, or you may be carrying anger from the past—with your father or other men. So you are willing to withhold from your own pleasure because "going for it" would be giving in to the person you're angry with.

Face the real issues, deal with your anger, and let yourself go for sex *for you*, even if he benefits. Try it. You'll be glad you did!

What if my mind wanders? Studies have shown that most women's minds wandered during sex. So we assume that is normal.

Today, studies have more carefully specified the effects of women's mind-wandering. Many times, it's a normal way women's minds work and isn't disruptive. Other times, thoughts of other things can get in the way of a positive sexual experience. It would be helpful to think about what happens for you during sex when your mind wanders.

Sometimes mind-wandering may add spark to your sexual time with your husband. If you go back to a special time the two of you enjoyed, that memory will likely increase your sensations in the moment. Your time may be enhanced by fantasizing the two of you in a more creative, special setting.

However, when your mind watches and evaluates how you are doing during sex (this is called spectatoring), performance anxiety sets in. Allowing your mind to wander to negative memories of the past or fears of pain or disappointment in the future will dampen your enjoyment and decrease your sexual pleasure.

The most common mind-wandering is remembering what you wanted to put on your grocery list or something you don't want to forget to tell your husband. Those are so normal, and neither helpful nor negative unless they distract from the moment.

"Perhaps the trick with our minds, as with many other things in life, is balance: There is a time for focus and a time for mind-wandering," writes Jenni Ogden. "We can control, to some extent, when our minds wander, and there are many situations where this is advantageous."[1]

The Two-Screen Method, a mindfulness approach developed by our associate Dr. Scott Symington,[2] is most helpful for getting your mind back to the focus of your sexual experience—your connection with your husband and with your body.

Imagine you are in a room with two screens. On the front screen, you are focusing on your sexual moments, enjoying closeness with your husband, the sensations of your body, the enjoyment of his body, lips to lips, and any other positive sensations you would add to the list. On the side screen are thoughts about things of the day, your to-do list, or negative interruptions to your enjoyment of the front screen.

When your mind drifts to the side screen, don't fight it or get frustrated with yourself for going there, just accept that it is there, but focus your attention back to the front screen and ride the waves of delight by keeping connected with your husband. Keep your eyes open and become actively engaged.

What if my husband keeps forgetting what I told him? He will! So remind him in a positive, inviting manner, and go after your desires with joy, rather than hoping he will remember. Don't play the game: "If he loves me, he will remember." His remembering or not remembering has nothing to do with love; he is wired differently from you.

What if we have sex the same way every time? Some couples enjoy what they have found works for them and don't vary much from that. Some of us are that way with food: Joyce could eat the same thing for breakfast the rest of her life; Cliff needs variety. So consider variety in your sexual lives in the same way. It's a choice that depends on what you enjoy.

What if quickies are all we ever have? Quickies can be fun, delightful, and even satisfying if they aren't the consistent diet. Even as a person can survive on fast food, most enjoy a somewhat regular gourmet delight or a good old-fashioned, healthy, home-cooked meal. Taking time to plan a sexual gourmet event will bring deeper intimacy and passion for both.

What if my or his sexual past has invaded our bedroom? Deal with that past outside of the bedroom. If the two of you have tried but have been unsuccessful in removing that past from your relationship, get help—the sooner the better. Past issues can poison your current love of each other and your enjoyment of sex together.

> Past issues can poison your enjoyment.

Once you have released that past and forgiven yourselves and each other, bask in God's grace and forgiveness. Then redo your bedroom and dedicate it to your relationship. Changes in your décor will reflect your new beginning. Invite God's blessing and commit yourselves to each other.

What if we don't talk about sex? If you haven't talked with your husband about sex yet, you must have jumped to this chapter before reading the others. Go back and read Chapter 6 out loud together. Establish a new approach to open communication about sex.

What if he doesn't turn me on? That isn't his job! However, that question, which we hear often, can have different meanings. If you mean, "I don't get aroused during sex with my husband," you will need to read Chapters 8 and 9 on healing hurts and dealing with hormonal issues or whatever might be preventing you from being able to become aroused.

If you mean, "I don't respond sexually to him anymore," you most likely have unrealistic expectations and have not made the shift from the initial attraction, which is dopamine driven, to a long-term attachment that is fueled by the brain chemical oxytocin.

Focus on making decisions about sex, creating the best conditions for the two of you, and going after your pleasure, although not in a way that takes away from your husband or is at his expense.

What if I'm not in love with him? Were you ever in love with your husband or did you marry without love? Are you looking for a feeling? How do you define love? If you are looking for a feeling, it might be that you are looking for that excited-love feeling that was there early on, as we mentioned in the previous answer.

Read 1 Corinthians 13 in several translations and in the paraphrase *The Message*. Then redefine love for your marriage. Seek help if you can't find love with your husband.

Keep Learning

As you've read this book, we hope you've learned that good sex doesn't just "happen" naturally. Instead, practicing, talking, and learning are the way to mutual satisfaction for you and your husband.

We are convinced that mutual sexual joy and fulfillment—to whatever degree is possible given a couple's situation and stage of life—is within your reach. This is possible as you take responsibility to do your part while releasing responsibility to your husband for his part.

Our calling is to help individuals and couples discover all they are as sexual persons designed in God's image and maximize the vitality their sexuality brings to all dimensions of their lives—in and out of bed.

What we've shared with you has come out of our rewarding work over more than forty years as we've helped individuals and couples find:

- new ways of communicating,
- real love for each other,
- more enjoyment, less pressure, and
- mutual satisfaction in their sexual relationship with each other.

And that's what we wish for you.

Remember to practice our Formula for Intimacy for fifteen minutes per day, including passionate kissing that does not lead to sex. Preserve the spark in your marriage by puckering up.

Embrace who you are as a sexual person designed in God's image! Sex is not about doing your duty. It's about pursuing all of who you are sexually, and sharing your sexual intensity, joy, and delight with your husband. Together, you can honor God as you create a sexual relationship that is a model of Christ and the church.

Above all, remember how God loves you, and strive to love your husband in the same way.

"Watch what God does, and then you do it. . . . Mostly what God does is love you. Keep company with him and learn a life of love. . . . He didn't love in order to get something from us but to give everything of himself to us. Love like that" (Ephesians 5:1-2).

Appendixes

Appendix 1A

Eating Plan for Hormonal Balance

BE SURE TO CONFIRM use of this plan with your physician. Basically, this plan is a low-carbohydrate, high-mineral, low-fat, and high-protein diet.

- Drink water before and between meals. Mineral water is great! To calculate the recommended number of ounces to drink daily, divide your weight in half to know how many ounces to drink. A 140-pound person would need 70 ounces of water per day.

- Eat small amounts frequently. Include protein.

- For oils, use olive oil, coconut oil, and grape-seed oil.

- Eat the equivalent of a cereal bowl of vegetables at lunch and one at dinner, including large quantities of green, leafy vegetables (preferably cooked, not raw).

- Eat one serving of whole grains per day, two servings of fruit per day, and unlimited amounts of berries and avocado.

- Ginger, turmeric, and cinnamon are recommended.

Eliminate or reduce:

- Sugar (all forms), artificial sweeteners, and syrup. You may use some pure maple syrup, molasses, and agave. Stevia is fine to use.
- White flour—all refined and processed flours.
- Coffee and black tea with caffeine (differing findings are reported on the benefits of caffeine, so be alert to what works for you); green tea and herbal teas are encouraged.
- Limit alcohol; limit wine to one glass (6 ounces) of red wine per day.
- Processed sausage, bacon, ham, cold cuts, and meats containing sweeteners or preservatives.
- Noodles, pasta, and white rice.
- Oranges, grapefruits, and other citrus fruits to keep a healthier acid-base balance.
- Consider eliminating cow's milk products (this is not necessary for all, but as we age, we decrease in enzyme production to digest dairy products). Sheep and goat's milk products are thought to be easier to digest due to the smaller casein molecules.
- *Possibly* omit gluten-containing grains and their derivatives: wheat, rye, barley.

Appendix 1B

Eating Plan Example

In the morning, drink a large glass of warm or room-temperature water.

BREAKFAST

- Eggs cooked with mushrooms and other vegetables, or turkey breakfast sausage/chicken-apple sausage, or nut butter on bread
- A half serving of whole grain bread or food starch, such as yams or other root vegetables, baked or sautéed
- Berries, especially blueberries
- Green tea (optional)

Sip water or tea between breakfast and snack.
Drink a large glass of water right before snack.

MID-MORNING NIBBLE

- Berries, half a green apple or other non-citrus fruit
- A nibble of protein—goat or sheep cheese, nuts, peanuts, or nut butters

Drink a large glass of water before lunch.

LUNCH

- Small amount of protein: chicken, salmon, tuna, pork, lamb, veal, venison, and nut butters are options
- Large amount of green vegetables steamed with cider vinegar or sautéed in coconut or olive oil. You may add a touch of balsamic vinegar for added taste.
- A half serving of whole grain bread or food starch (or full serving for breakfast)—yams, carrots, parsnips, potato, or other

Sip water or tea between lunch and snack.
Drink a large glass of water right before snack.

AFTERNOON NIBBLE

- One fruit, unlimited berries, cherries and/or avocado or veggies with guacamole
- A nibble of protein, nuts, or quinoa bar

Drink water between snack and dinner.
Drink a large glass of water before dinner.

DINNER (KEEP LIGHT)

- Animal protein: fish, chicken, salmon, tuna, pork, lamb, veal, and venison are good
- Vegetables, especially dark green such as kale or spinach, steamed (or sautéed in coconut oil)
- No starch

An example of a healthy choice for dinner is a home-cooked soup made with vegetables and bone-in meat with a touch of cider vinegar, and a green apple.

Choose a noncaffeinated tea in the evening, such as rooibos tea or other herbal tea.

EVENING NIBBLE
(Optional—some sleep better with a snack; others rest better without any food in the evening.)

- Vegetables dipped in guacamole or hummus

Appendix 1C

Supplements Suggested for Menopausal/Postmenopausal Women

TAKE SUPPLEMENTS WITH YOUR PHYSICIAN'S APPROVAL.

- Probiotic to improve gut health and enhance absorption and benefits of supplements
- Black cohosh, 60 mg daily (Although it has had mixed reviews, the benefits in reducing hot flashes are reported by many women.)
- DHEA (dehydroepiandrosterone—10 mg, not more!); take in the morning to support hormonal balance
- A well-balanced vitamin/mineral supplement, including 400 IU of vitamin E; 50 mg of B_6; 800 mcg of folic acid per day; take as directed
- Vitamin D_3—at least 3000 IU; take in the evening
- Calcium, magnesium balanced in a ratio of about two to one (typically 1250 mg calcium and 650–700 mg magnesium, spread out so that about a third is taken midday and two-thirds at bedtime with the D_3 suggested above)
- Flaxseed oil or another source of omega-3 oil
- CoQ_{10} as directed
- Try using a digestive enzyme before eating a food that is difficult for you to digest (Often as people age, dairy products are difficult to digest, and this may help.)

Appendix 2A

Clinical Genital Examination

READ ALOUD TOGETHER and discuss any fears or needs for safety. Then follow the steps.

STEP 1: Have diagrams of the male genitalia and the female external genitalia. Have a hand mirror and adequate lighting available.

STEP 2: Shower or bathe together; lather up each other's bodies and enjoy the pleasure and relaxation of touching each other in that process, not for the purpose of arousal.

STEP 3: In a private, well-lit room, with the diagram of male genitalia, the husband identifies all the specific parts of the penis and testes. If it is comfortable for both, the husband may invite the wife to join in the exploration by touching various parts as they are identified. Wife, only participate to the extent that it is comfortable for you. Particularly note the coronal ridge and the frenulum, or seam, on the back side of the penis. After exploring the various parts of the genitals, talk about what kind of touch feels good, any stimulation of the genitals your partner has given you in the past that you would like more of, and any stimulation or handling of the genitals that has been unpleasant for you. Wife, talk about ways you enjoy pleasuring his genitals and any feelings of discomfort you have with the male genitals.

STEP 4: Wife, assume a comfortable position with legs spread apart, light on the genitals, diagram within view, and the hand mirror between the legs so you can see the genitals clearly. Identify for your husband how your outer labia come together. Then you spread the outer labia and identify the inner labia. Find and show him the clitoris, and how the labia form a hood over the clitoris. Identify for him the shaft of the clitoris, almost like a hidden, small penis up behind the tip of the clitoris. Touch the tip, or glans, of the clitoris and then the areas around it, and talk with your husband about what kind of touch feels good and where. If it is comfortable for both, invite your husband to join in exploration and touching as is comfortable.

Identify the urinary meatus, vaginal opening, and any other points of interest. Talk about what genital stimulation your partner has given you in the past that has felt good, what you would like more of, what touching has been negative, and how stimulation of your genitals might be enhanced. Husband, talk about ways you enjoy pleasuring her genitals and any feelings of discomfort you have with the female genitalia. When genital touching has not been comfortable for a woman, many times it has been too direct. Experiment with putting a flat hand over the pons and the pointer and middle fingers along the labia.

STEP 5: You may write your reactions and then talk about what this has felt like for each of you, what was comfortable or uncomfortable, and what you learned about yourselves and each other.

This is a clinical learning experience, not for the purpose of arousal. If arousal should occur, it is okay. But do not focus on it; ignore it or enjoy it without pursuing it.

Appendix 2B

Non-Demand Teaching

PREPARE THE SETUP: pillows against the headboard of the bed usually work best. Design this for teaching, rather than for arousal and release. Arousal and release are involuntary responses. If those responses should happen, enjoy them, but that is not the goal or focus of this exercise.

Bathe or shower together in a way that brings relaxation and enjoyment of each other's bodies, not touching for the purpose of stimulation or arousal.

The woman starts the experience by sitting in front of her husband in the non-demand position (upper of the two diagrams). She places her hands over his hands and uses his hands to caress her face, breasts, abdomen and genitals. Guiding the hands can feel awkward. If so, talk and guide. The purpose of the exercise is for the woman to discover, guide, and teach her husband what kind of touch she likes. This is a good time for both husband and wife to experiment and communicate about the kind of genital touch that is enjoyable. This is not necessarily an arousing experience, but a clinical teaching. However, if arousal should occur, enjoy it.

Reverse roles so that the husband guides his wife's hands to discover and teach the touch he enjoys on the upper front of his body. He may need to slide down and use a modified version of the upper diagram. When he is guiding his wife in caressing his lower body, especially the genitals, we would encourage the use of the lower diagram. A lubricant or oil may enhance the experience.

Talk about what you learned in this experience, as well as anything else that you've always enjoyed or has always been painful or difficult for either or both of you.

Appendix 3

Problem-Solving Initiation Issues

A. Each write how you experience your sexual initiation pattern. What do you do and what do you feel? (Use "I" statements; avoid "you" statements.)

B. During a prescheduled one- to two-hour block of time:

   1. Read your experience of the problem to your husband; then he reads his experience of the problem to you.
   2. Describe how you understand your husband's experience; he does the same for you.
   3. Clarify any message that was misunderstood.
   4. Discuss and agree on any need for change.
   5. Make a plan.

C. Suggested plan.

   1. Select one or two weeks during which:
      a. Usual initiator makes no hint at sexual activity, but is loving and warm.
      b. Usual avoider is responsible to initiate one sexual event of his or her choice.

2. Have time set aside at the end of this designated time to:
   a. Talk about your feelings and your husband's feelings that occurred during the week(s).
   b. Talk about what actually happened sexually.
   c. Make a follow-up plan for the next week or two.
   d. Revise the plan to accommodate any difficulties that occurred.

Appendix 4

Sample Letter for Requesting a Hormone Panel

Date: _____

To Dr. _____:
We are requesting that a hormone panel be done on
_____. In understanding the total picture
regarding her current symptoms, it would be most helpful to obtain
the following:

- Estrogen levels
- Progesterone level
- Total testosterone
- Free testosterone*
- DHEA-S
- SHBG

*Many laboratories fail to obtain a free (or bioavailable)
testosterone level. It is necessary to assess the free testosterone in
relation to the total in order to adequately determine if hormone
levels are contributing to her concerns.

Thank you for participating in this recommendation. Please
e-mail the results to Joyce Penner at penners@attglobal.net.
Sincerely,
Joyce J. Penner, M.N., R.N.
Clinical Nurse Specialist/Sex Therapist

Notes

CHAPTER 1: ENJOY

1. Michael Castleman, "Attention, Ladies: Semen Is an Antidepressant," *All about Sex* (blog), *Psychology Today*, January 31, 2001, https://www.psychologytoday.com/blog/all-about-sex/201101/attention-ladies-semen-is-antidepressant.
2. Judith Sachs, *The Healing Power of Sex* (Bloomington, IN: iUniverse, 2008).
3. Clifford L. Penner and Joyce J. Penner, *Getting Your Sex Life Off to a Great Start* (Nashville: Nelson, 1994).
4. Cindy Hazan and Phillip Shaver, "Romantic Love Conceptualized as an Attachment Process," *Journal of Personality and Social Psychology* 52, no. 3 (1987): 511–524.
5. Robert J. Sternberg and Michael L. Barnes, eds., *The Psychology of Love* (New Haven, CT: Yale University Press, 1988).
6. Gregory L. Jantz, *The Body God Designed: How to Love the Body You've Got While You Get the Body You Want* (Lake Mary, FL: Siloam, 2007).
7. Ibid., 12.
8. Clifford L. Penner and Joyce J. Penner, *What Every Wife Wants Her Husband to Know about Sex* (Nashville: Nelson, 1998), 37.
9. Penner and Penner, *What Every Wife Wants Her Husband to Know about Sex*, 49.

CHAPTER 2: LISTEN

1. William H. Masters and Virginia E. Johnson, "Human Sexual Response: Function and Dysfunction," Six-Day Intensive Postgraduate Workshop (St. Louis, MO: Reproductive Biology Research Foundation, October 20–25, 1975).
2. Ibid.
3. Louann Brizendine, *The Female Brain* (New York: Broadway Books, 2006), 79.
4. Gillian Einstein, ed., *Sex and the Brain* (Cambridge, MA: MIT Press, 2007).
5. Clifford L. Penner and Joyce J. Penner, *Restoring the Pleasure: Complete*

Step-by-Step Programs to Help Couples Overcome the Most Common Sexual Barriers (Nashville: W Publishing Group, 2016).

6. Brizendine, *The Female Brain*, 3. Also see Appendix One: "The Female Brain and Hormone Therapy," 165–180.

7. Barry Komisaruk, "Pain Brain Regions Also Active during Female Orgasm." Presented at the Society for Neuroscience Annual Meeting, San Diego, November 15, 2010.

8. Brizendine, *The Female Brain*, "The Female Brain and Postpartum Depression," 181–183.

9. Stephanie Bender and Treacy Colbert, *End Your Menopause Misery: The 10-Day Self-Care Plan* (San Francisco: Conari Press, 2013).

10. "Hormone Therapy: Is It Right for You?" Mayo Clinic, accessed February 4, 2017, http://www.mayoclinic.org/diseases-conditions/menopause/in-depth /hormone-therapy/art-20046372.

11. Recommended are 150 minutes of moderate exercise or 75 minutes of vigorous exercise, or an equivalent mix spread out over a week. See "Exercise and Fitness," *Harvard Health Publications*, accessed February 4, 2017, www.health.harvard.edu /topics/exercise-and-fitness.

12. Paula Rinehart, *Strong Women, Soft Hearts* (Nashville: Nelson, 2005).

CHAPTER 3: LEAD

1. "How to Do PC Muscle Exercises," *WikiHow*, http://www.wikihow.com/Do-PC -Muscle-Exercises.

2. "G-spot," *Wikipedia*, last modified January 23, 2017, https://en.wikipedia.org /wiki/G-spot.

CHAPTER 4: PLAN AND PREPARE

1. Kerstin Uvnäs Moberg, *The Oxytocin Factor* (Boston: Da Capo Press, 2011), 57–60.

2. Formula for Intimacy cards available at www.passionatecommitment.com.

3. Amy Muise, Ulrich Schimmack, and Emily A. Impett, "Sexual Frequency Predicts Greater Well-Being, But More Is Not Always Better," *Social Psychological and Personality Science* 7, no. 4 (November 18, 2015).

CHAPTER 5: PLEASURE

1. Adapted from Penner and Penner, *Restoring the Pleasure*, 146–196.

2. Ibid., 148.

CHAPTER 6: TALK

1. Information in this section is adapted from Clifford L. Penner and Joyce J. Penner, *Restoring the Pleasure* (Nashville: Thomas Nelson, 2016). Used with permission.

2. Toni Weschler, *Taking Charge of Your Fertility, 20th Anniversary Edition: The*

Definitive Guide to Natural Birth Control, Pregnancy Achievement, and Reproductive Health (New York: William Morrow, 2015).

3. Visit www.womentowomen.com to take the hormone health assessment.

CHAPTER 7: PRACTICE INTIMACY

1. Ian Kerner, *Passionista: The Empowered Woman's Guide to Pleasuring a Man* (New York: William Morrow, 2008), xxi.
2. Clifford L. Penner and Joyce J. Penner, *The Married Guy's Guide to Great Sex* (Carol Stream, IL: Tyndale, 2017), 73.
3. Penner and Penner, *Restoring the Pleasure*.
4. Robert Weiss (founder of the Sexual Recovery Institute in Los Angeles, CA), "Do You Have an Intimacy Disorder?" interview at www.itscheating.com/intimacy/do-you-have-an-intimacy-disorder-vixely-talks-to-expert-robert-weiss/.
5. Mark Laaser (Christian sexual addiction specialist), workshops in Minnesota, https://www.faithfulandtrue.com.
6. Allan Schore, University of California, Los Angeles, lecture at Fuller Theological Seminary, Pasadena, CA.

CHAPTER 8: PURSUE HEALING

1. Celebrate Recovery is "a biblical and balanced program that helps us overcome our hurts, hang-ups, and habits." See www.celebraterecovery.com.
2. Paul Tournier, *Guilt and Grace: A Psychological Study* (New York: HarperCollins, 1982).
3. Penner and Penner, *Restoring the Pleasure*, 290–310.
4. To find a pelvic floor physical therapist, go to www.pelvicpain.org, www.ic-network.com, or http://www.apta.org.
5. For further information on genital self-examination, visit http://www.webmd.com/women/vaginal-self-examination-vse; http://www.ourbodiesourselves.org/health-info/self-exam-vulva-vagina; and http://www.soc.ucsb.edu/sexinfo/article/female-genital-self-exam.
6. Penner and Penner, *Restoring the Pleasure*.

CHAPTER 9: EMBRACE DIFFERENCES

1. "A Different Voice of Carol Gilligan," from Em Griffin, *A First Look at Communication Theory*, 1st ed. (New York: McGraw-Hill, 1991), https://courses.soe.ucsc.edu/courses/cmpe80e/Spring14/01/attachments/26751.
2. Steve Biddulph, *Raising Boys: Why Boys Are Different—and How to Help Them Become Happy and Well-Balanced Men*, 3rd ed. (Emeryville, CA: Ten Speed Press, 2014).
3. Barton Goldsmith, "Emotional Fitness," *Psychology Today*, August 31, 2010.
4. Róisín Parkins, "Gender and Emotional Expressiveness: An Analysis of Prosodic Features in Emotional Expression," *Griffith Working Papers in Pragmatics and Intercultural Communication* 5, no. 1 (2012): 46–54.

5. John M. Gottman and Nan Silver, *The Seven Principles for Making Marriage Work* (New York: Harmony Books, 2015), 32.
6. Ellie Lisitsa, "The Four Horsemen: The Antidotes," The Gottman Institute blog, accessed February 4, 2017, https://www.gottman.com/blog/the-four-horsemen-the-antidotes.

CHAPTER 11: ACCEPT REALITY
1. Harville Hendrix, *Getting the Love You Want: A Guide for Couples*, 20th anniversary ed. (New York: Henry Holt, 2007).

CHAPTER 12: KEEP LEARNING
1. Jenni Ogden, "Why Our Minds Wander" *Psychology Today*, January 21, 2015.
2. Scott Symington, "Two-Screen Method," YouTube video, 6:24, posted April 8, 2015, https://www.youtube.com/watch?v=H3FEMbMXv6Q.

Additional Resources

Dillow, Linda, and Dr. Juli Slattery. *Passion Pursuit: What Kind of Love Are You Making?* Moody Publishers, 2013.

Jantz, Gregory L., Ph.D. *The Body God Designed: How to Love the Body You've Got While You Get the Body You Want.* Siloam, 2007.

Parrott, Les, and Leslie Parrott, *L.O.V.E.: Putting Your Love Styles to Work for You.* Zondervan, 2009.

Penner, Clifford, Ph.D., and Joyce Penner, M.N. *Restoring the Pleasure.* Word Publishing. 1994.

Penner, Clifford, Ph.D., and Joyce Penner, M.N. *The Married Guy's Guide to Great Sex.* A Focus on the Family book published by Tyndale House Publishers, 2017.

Rinehart, Paula. *Sex and the Soul of a Woman.* Zondervan, 2004.

Rinehart, Paula. *Strong Women; Soft Hearts: A Woman's Guide to Cultivating a Wise Heart and a Passionate Life.* Word Publishing, 2001.

Thomas, Angela. *Do You Think I'm Beautiful?* Nelson Books, 2003.

About the Authors

BECOMING CHRISTIAN "sexperts" was never our intention. Our "calling" started forty-one years ago at Lake Avenue Church (LAC) in Pasadena, California, which we began attending in 1965 while Cliff attended the Graduate School of Psychology at Fuller Seminary.

Cliff was asked to talk to young mothers at LAC about teaching kids about sex. At that time, Cliff had a private practice as a clinical psychologist and Joyce had been teaching nursing at California State University Los Angeles and was in charge of curriculum development for the new nursing program at Azusa Pacific University.

A Fuller student wife who attended Cliff's talk asked him to teach a ten-week class on sexual adjustment in marriage for the wives of Fuller Seminary students. He told her he had said all he knew in forty-five minutes. She prevailed, Cliff insisted that Joyce join him, and we prepared and presented the classes in the spring of 1975. The information made a significant difference in those women's sexual relationships with their husbands. We pursued training to keep up with the requests we received to teach, write, and provide sex therapy.

We continue to work as certified sex therapists with couples and individuals, lead couples' seminars for sexual enhancement in marriage, and train other therapists and counselors around the world. Working together in this specialty continues to be a most rewarding journey and is a great way to spend this stage of our lives—traveling and training others to "do what we do"—to use the words of Cliff's mother, who could never use the "s" word.

Sex Matters!

As a husband, you can create greater
love and passion in the bedroom.

FOCUS ON THE FAMILY®

Welcome to the Family

Whether you purchased this book, borrowed it, or received it as a gift, thanks for reading it! This is just one of many insightful, biblically based resources that Focus on the Family produces for people in all stages of life.

Focus is a global Christian ministry dedicated to helping families thrive as they celebrate and cultivate God's design for marriage and experience the adventure of parenthood. Our outreach exists to support individuals and families in the joys and challenges they face, and to equip and empower them to be the best they can be.

Through our many media outlets, we offer help and hope, promote moral values and share the life-changing message of Jesus Christ with people around the world.

Focus on the Family MAGAZINES

These faith-building, character-developing publications address the interests, issues, concerns, and challenges faced by every member of your family from preschool through the senior years.

FOCUS ON THE FAMILY®	FOCUS ON THE FAMILY CLUBHOUSE®	FOCUS ON THE FAMILY CLUBHOUSE JR.®	FOCUS ON THE FAMILY BRIO™	FOCUS ON THE FAMILY CITIZEN®
Marriage & Parenting	Ages 8 to 12	Ages 3 to 7	Teen Girls	U.S. News Issues

For More INFORMATION

 ONLINE:
Log on to
FocusOnTheFamily.com/magazines
In Canada, log on to
FocusOnTheFamily.ca

 PHONE:
Call toll-free:
**800-A-FAMILY
(232-6459)**
In Canada, call toll-free:
800-661-9800

CP0552

Rev. 6/17

More Resources to Help You Thrive in Marriage and Life

Crazy *Little Thing* Called *Marriage*

12 Secrets *for a* Lifelong Romance

DR. GREG & ERIN SMALLEY

FOREWORD BY GARY CHAPMAN

Starting now, this could be your best day, week, month, or year! Discover ways to express your needs, embrace your purpose, and love more fully. We offer life-transforming books, e-books, videos, devotionals, study guides, audiobooks, and audio dramas to equip you for God's calling on your life. Visit your favorite retailer, or go to **FocusOnTheFamily.com/resources**.

CP1037